Business Writing for Results

How to Create a Sense of Urgency and Increase Response to All of Your Business Communications

JANE K. CLELAND

McGraw-Hill

New York   Chicago   San Francisco   Lisbon   London   Madrid   Mexico City
Milan   New Delhi   San Juan   Seoul   Singapore   Sydney   Toronto

Library of Congress Cataloging-in-Publication Data

Cleland, Jane K.
    Business writing for results : how to create a sense of urgency and increase response
to all of your business communications / Jane K. Cleland.
        p.   cm.
    Includes index.
    ISBN 0-07-140570-4
    1. Commercial correspondence—Handbooks, manuals, etc.   2. Business writing—
Handbooks, manuals, etc.   3. English language—Business English—Handbooks,
manuals, etc. I. Title.

    HF5726 .C56   2003
    651.7′4—dc21   2002026329

1 2 3 4 5 6 7 8 9 0   DOC/DOC   2 1 0 9 8 7 6 5 4 3

ISBN 0-07-140570-4

McGraw-Hill books are available at special quantity discounts to use as premiums and sales
promotions, or for use in corporate training programs. For more information, please write to
the Director of Special Sales, Professional Publishing, McGraw-Hill, Two Penn Plaza, New York,
NY 10121-2298. Or contact your local bookstore.

This book is printed on acid-free paper.

My father, a non-native speaker,
struggled to make himself understood in English.
He often wished for simple ways to
remember complex writing rules so that
he could produce professional letters quickly and easily.
This book is for my father.

Contents

Introduction

Malcolm Forbes once said, "A good business letter can get you a job interview, get you off the hook, or get you money. It's totally asinine to blow your chances of getting whatever you want with a business letter that turns people off instead of turning them on."

Here's the bottom line: If you can't produce well-written communications, it's unlikely you'll achieve business success. No matter what your industry, no matter what your job, no matter what other business abilities are required to succeed in your career, you must be able to get your points across clearly and persuasively in writing. Writing well in business involves more than merely following the rules of grammar. It requires a keen understanding of two things:

1. Your objective—what do you want your readers to do as a result of reading your material?
2. Your target audience—what is going to motivate your readers to do whatever it is you want them to do?

Most business professionals understand that the ability to communicate clearly and concisely is not an optional business skill—it's a *critical* one. What they usually haven't considered is that *business* writing is a different kind of writing from the writing they learned in school. It's neither academic nor informal. It differs from technical writing, creative writing, and journalism. Just as each of these writing styles has standards unique to it, so too is business writing unique. At its best, it's conversational without being chatty, accessible without being too familiar, clear without being overly simplistic, and professional without being stuffy. This book sets out an easy-to-use and easy-to-understand three-step system *guaranteed* to help readers write business communications well.

INFLUENCE DECISION-MAKERS AND GET THE RESPONSE YOU WANT

Through case studies, examples, and hands-on exercises, you will learn to use my three-step model to respond in all media. You'll read examples that reflect the kind of writing you do every day—from E-mails and the Web to traditional reports, from sales letters to collection letters, and from proposals to memos.

Specifically, you will learn to write:

- E-mail subject lines that get your messages opened ahead of the pack
- proposals that persuade others to your point of view
- memos and letters that express your ideas succinctly
- Web copy that encourages interactivity
- workbooks and training materials that motivate students to learn
- reports that influence decision-makers

You'll learn strategies to adapt the valuable guidelines and techniques used by today's most successful business writers. Through exercises and lively debriefings, you'll discover how to write *persuasively*. Whatever the media, you'll know how to achieve these critical business objectives:

1. Motivate readers to specific action (for example, "request a personalized quote" or "call for further information").
2. Create just the image you seek to convey (*conservative and professional*, for instance, or *informal and playful*).
3. Write error-free documents in one-third less time. (By following the three-step system, the writing process is streamlined.)
4. Catch even the hardest-to-find mistakes. (Specific proofing tactics go beyond the basics; not only will typos and the like be found, but learning to fix common errors encourages critical evaluation.)
5. Avoid common mistakes that undermine individual and organizational credibility (such as run-on sentences and improper punctuation).
6. Rivet readers' attention to get E-mails and letters opened and read (by providing meaningful information in the subject line of an E-mail or in the opening line of a letter, for example).

Everyone who writes for business will benefit from this book. Experienced writers will enjoy a refresher course and pick up dozens of time-saving tips. Novices will learn an approach proven to quickly and efficiently generate written communications. You will learn everything you need to know to get your ideas across clearly and persuasively. Through exercises and practice—and by reading alternative solutions to the exercises—you'll learn how to use my tried-and-true three-step model to dramatically improve your writing.

A METHODICAL SYSTEM THAT PRODUCES RESULTS

By dividing the task of writing into three distinct steps, you'll find the process of writing easier and discover shortcuts that will save you time. The three steps are:

Step One: Get Your Thoughts in Order
Step Two: Create a Draft on Paper (or on Your Computer)
Step Three: Revise for Clarity

Within each chapter, there are several exercises. Intended to ensure that you practice using the tools, the exercises are challenging and fun. Additionally, the exercises will help you:

- prove to yourself that you'll be able to remember and use the three-step model
- know that there are always several ways to express a thought; this tip helps you avoid writer's block as you hunt for the one "right" way to write something
- save time and energy while still producing top-notch writing; no more will you be dependent on the "aha" of creative inspiration

Each chapter uses specific techniques to elicit the information needed to write well. This approach, therefore, becomes a checklist for you as you go through the writing process. Over time, you'll discover that the more frequently you consult the checklist, the more quickly the system will become second nature.

The checklist includes:

Step One: Get Your Thoughts in Order

- ✓ Answer the question, "What do I want my readers to do as a result of reading this?"
- ✓ Analyze your audience by considering their personalities and by using the Formality Index.
- ✓ Assess your writing assignment with the Matrix of Persuasion.

Step Two: Create a Draft on Paper (or on Your Computer)

- ✓ Organize your thoughts.
- ✓ Use the Hub & Spokes model to get your thoughts on paper. Once done, select your beginning and ending paragraphs.
- ✓ Generate a first draft.

Step Three: Revise for Clarity

- ✓ Revise to a second draft with the Empathy Index, and focus on the lead and salutation.
- ✓ Add a snappy close. (And consider adding a P.S., addendum, appendix, enclosures, or attachments.)
- ✓ Make the writing specific.
- ✓ Select the best words using the principle of FURY.
- ✓ Ensure the writing is concise, clear, positive, and parallel.
- ✓ Check your grammar, punctuation, word usage, and capitalization.
- ✓ Make the draft visually appealing.
- ✓ Read the entire draft.

A SYSTEM TESTED AND PROVEN TO WORK

Attendees at my various writing seminars report that my three-step writing system works. In the twelve years I've been speaking on this subject, refining my systems and methods, more than ten thousand people have attended my programs; their successes prove my methods work and attest to the fact that you will benefit, too. No matter how good or poor your writing is now, you'll learn to write better, more clearly, and more persuasively—and you'll do it in less time.

CHAPTER ONE

Arrange Your Thoughts

A METHODICAL PROCESS

Writing for results requires encouraging your readers to take action. In this chapter, you'll learn how to arrange your thoughts so that you write with the action in mind. When you think first and then write, you have a much better chance of achieving your objective.

You're going to learn a methodical process, one that will be easy to use and easy to remember. In this chapter, you're going to use three tools that, taken together, will help you set your objective and analyze your audience. The three tools are:

1. Answer the question, "What do I want my readers to do as a result of reading this?"
2. Analyze your audience by considering their personalities and using the Formality Index.
3. Assess your writing assignment with the Matrix of Persuasion.

SET ACTION OBJECTIVES

The first tool in writing for response is knowing exactly what you want your readers to do as a result of reading your material. Determining an action objective makes writing easier and more straightforward. Keeping the end result in your mind as you write enables you to aim for it. When you know where you're heading, you're more likely to get there.

Let's say, for example, that your boss has asked you to organize the summer picnic. You've selected the venue and need to announce it. You decide to send an E-mail to everyone in the company. Consider these two objectives:

1. I want to inform employees about the date of the summer picnic.

2. I want employees to RSVP regarding the summer picnic by the fifteenth of the month.

To get people to RSVP, you need to inform them of the date; however, simply informing the employees in no way motivates them to act.

An action objective focuses on the response you hope to elicit; a passive objective focuses on you or your goals. An action objective, for example, states, "to confirm via E-mail," whereas a passive objective states, "to understand my points."

Every time you identify a passive objective (such as, "to inform"), convert it into an action objective ("to RSVP," for instance). The easiest way to do this is to ask yourself the question, "Why do I care?"

In this example, posing the question to yourself would elicit an answer that leads directly to the desired action:

I want to inform employees about the date of the summer picnic.

Why do I care if they're informed? Because . . .

I want employees to RSVP regarding the summer picnic by the fifteenth of the month.

If you send your boss an E-mail updating him (or her) that you've scheduled a meeting for next Tuesday, you may think your objective is to update him on the progress you've made.

But "to update" is a passive objective. Convert it into an action objective by asking yourself, "Why do I care if he is updated?" Your answer may be:

I want my boss to *tell* me I'm doing a good job.

I want my boss to *ask* me to let him know how the meeting went.

2

I want my boss to *congratulate* me on having succeeded in scheduling the meeting.

All of these statements are action oriented; you want your boss to *do* something—in this example, to *tell, ask,* or *congratulate*. Knowing the action you seek makes the entire writing process easier.

Sometimes you desire an action objective that aims to avoid a negative consequence. In this example, when you ask yourself, "Why do I care about updating my boss?" you may respond:

I don't want my boss to ask me for an update; I want him to perceive that I'm on top of things.

Read each of the scenarios in Exercise 1 and write an action objective that best describes what each person wants his or her reader(s) to do. If you find you're writing a passive objective, ask yourself, "Why do I care?" to help you transform the passive objective into an action objective.

Following each scenario are examples of well-written objectives. Keep in mind that there are many good variations. If the objective you write allows you to envision a reader doing something, it's a well-written objective. On the other hand, if your objective describes a feeling or thought, or if it expresses an intention, it's not likely to be effective. As you practice writing objectives and evaluate your work, think action!

EXERCISE 1: *Write a One-Sentence Objective*

1. Justin's company has an intranet that posts openings within the company and all its subsidiaries worldwide. Justin wants to apply for a new position within his business unit. The job he's interested in represents a promotion and would move him up to the same level as his current boss. Company policy requires that job applications include a letter of support from the employee's current supervisor. Justin has decided to send an E-mail to his boss as a first step in putting together his application for the new job.

Write a one-sentence objective for Justin's E-mail.

Justin's action objectives might include:

- "To receive an E-mail from my boss that enthusiastically endorses my job application."
- "To get a phone call from my boss to schedule a time to meet and discuss my job application."

2. Mariana, vice president of a telecommunications firm, has received a letter of complaint from a customer. The customer reports that he was treated rudely by Norman, a customer satisfaction team member. Mariana wants to gather information before responding to the customer's letter and decides to make her request in writing. She plans to E-mail Norman directly and copy his boss.

Write a one-sentence objective for Mariana's E-mail.

Mariana's action objectives might include:

- "To receive from Norman a written explanation of his conduct within twenty-four hours."
- "To have the customer's records forwarded to me by Norman's direct supervisor by the end of business today."

3. Philip is a volunteer at a crisis hot line center in his community. He has joined a 10-kilometer walk-a-thon for the hot line; every person he signs up agrees to donate one dollar for every kilometer that he completes. He decides to create a small flyer and slide it under the doors of the residents in his apartment building.

Write a one-sentence objective for Philip's flyer.

Philip's action objectives might include:

- "To receive signed pledges under my door this week."
- "To get 'way to go' notes of support, in addition to the signed pledges, under my door this week."

4. Tawana owns and operates a small bookkeeping service. Business is good, and she decides to send out sales letters in an attempt to grow her business.

Write a one-sentence objective for Tawana's letter.

Tawana's action objectives might include:

- "To receive phone calls from potential customers requesting more information."
- "To receive phone calls from potential customers signing up for my bookkeeping service."

As you write action objectives, keep alert for passive language. In general, avoid words that are not specifically action oriented, such as:

- educate
- motivate
- inspire
- inform
- update

Instead, use words and phrases that are directive and action oriented, such as:

- Call and reserve your place at . . .
- Write for further information . . .
- Attend the meeting . . .
- E-mail your staff . . .
- Complete the form . . .

Once you have a clear, action-oriented objective, you're ready to go on to the second step: targeting your specific readers.

ANALYZE YOUR TARGET READERS

In order to create the sense of urgency needed to get your target readers to take the action that you want them to take, you need to understand their needs and wants, and you need to address them with the proper level of formality. Together, these two steps—understanding what's likely to motivate your readers and identifying the appropriate level of formality—enable you to write to your specific audience; these steps comprisse the second tool of this chapter.

Before you write, you need to think about what thoughts, beliefs, emotions, or ideas are meaningful to your target readers. You need to be able to answer the question "Why would they do what I'm asking?" Given that what will inspire one person to act may not motivate someone else, it's important that you look at the situation from your specific readers' points of view—not your own—and identify what represents a benefit to those readers.

Consider the difference between features and benefits. A feature belongs to the product or service. A benefit belongs to the user of the product or service. People respond to benefits, not features. For example, let's say you want to write a flyer offering a discount on purchases of your grass seed.

Features: the size, weight, color, and category of the grass seed
General Benefit: how quickly your lawn will grow
Specific Benefits: Your lawn will be:

- lush and green
- easy to care for
- the envy of your neighbors
- great for croquet and badminton

Consider how each specific benefit is likely to speak to a different kind of person. Some people want a beautiful lawn; others would like a beautiful lawn, but only if it's easy to care for. Still others want a lawn that will impress people, while others are only interested in a lawn for what it provides—a play area. There's no right or wrong. There's no one best benefit. People are different from one another. In order for your writing to generate results, you need to know enough about your target readers to be able to figure out which benefits will motivate them to act.

There are various ways to categorize people. For instance, you could evaluate their demographics (such as age or gender). Or you could assess psychographic factors (for instance, their lifestyle or socioeconomic status). In writing, one of the most useful approaches is to consider your target readers' personality types. Doing so enables you to select words and phrases that are likely to motivate your target audience to action.

While there are many models that describe personality, the following model is easy to use and easy to remember. Consider the differences among the four personality types below. I call them the Accommodator, the Optimist, the Producer, and the Data Collector.

- The Accommodator likes people but prefers small groups. Accommodators are kind, gentle, calm, methodical, and prudent. They are caretakers and tend to work in jobs that allow them to be helpers.
- The Optimist is sunny in spirit, impulsive, dramatic, fun, articulate, emotional, and sensitive. Optimists are party animals. They are creative and tend to work in jobs that allow them to interact with a lot of people and use their creative flair.
- The Producer is impatient, focused, ambitious, goal oriented, competitive, and intolerant of people's foibles. Producers are terrific problem-solvers. They are doers and tend to work in jobs that allow them to work toward a clearly understood goal.
- The Data Collector is independent, self-reliant, rational, curious, systematic, and self-contained. Data Collectors love research. They are fact oriented and tend to work in jobs that require attention to detail.

While most people are a mixture of all four personality types, most people also tend to demonstrate the attributes of one or another of the personality types in various environments and gravitate to jobs that suit their personality. Thus knowing someone's job can help you identify their personality type. As a writer, you can reach logical conclusions about which words and phrases to use based on people's jobs.

For example, which of the four personality types would most likely enjoy being a hospital nurse? The job requires patient care and follow-up, the ability to empathize, and the skill to explain complex procedures in an understanding and kind manner.

Isn't it likely that a nurse will be an Accommodator? An Accommodator is giving, gentle, and likes helping other people. If you're trying to motivate a nurse to participate in a continuing education conference, for example, it makes sense to stress the benefits of helping, because helping is a prime motivator to an Accommodator.

How about a graphic designer in an advertising agency? The job requires that the designer come up with new ideas and clever approaches, work happily on tight deadlines, and socialize with clients.

Did you recognize the Optimist? An Optimist is creative, social, and works well under pressure. If you're writing an E-mail to remind the graphic designer to fill out his or her health benefit update form, you should use language targeting the Optimist and highlight the benefit of filling it out promptly and not having to think about it again.

How about a senior executive? The job requires the ability to focus on the goal of raising shareholder value above all else, quick and confident decision making, and problem solving.

Did you recognize the Producer? A Producer is goal and bottom-line oriented, and is motivated by getting things done. If you're trying to solicit money for a nonprofit organization from a Producer, for example, it makes sense to highlight the bottom-line benefit of the nonprofit group.

How about someone working alone in a laboratory evaluating slides of blood samples and recording the results in a ledger?

Did you recognize that a Data Collector is likely to love that job? It's task and fact oriented, procedural, and rational. Thus if you're writing a newsletter article trying to motivate a lab technician to adhere to a new safety policy, you'd want to use words that speak directly to a Data Collector by focusing on the details of the new policy.

Take a look at Table 1.1. Do you see how the recommended words and phrases match each personality? The words and phrases are intended to help you begin the process of targeting different people. They are not intended to be a complete listing but rather to serve as a guide.

Not only will the words and phrases in Table 1.1 help you motivate people, they will also help you motivate groups. This flexibility is critical when your communication needs to reach multiple audience segments or a broad base where it's impossible to identify personality, or when you know all personality types will be represented—members of your community, visitors to your website, or all employees, for example. It's a very common dilemma that either you can't figure out a person's personality typeor there's a mixture and you are uncertain which type to target.

For example, let's say that your company is trying to encourage all employees to use their personal digital assistant (PDA). The company has provided training on using the new PDA; now you need to send an E-mail to all employees reminding them of the benefits.

Table 1.1 Word and Phrase Guide to Personality

Following are words and phrases that are likely to motivate each personality type.

Accommodator	Optimist	Producer	Data Collector
help	fun	get it done	data
need support	wacky	hurry up	analysis
feedback	offbeat	stop complaining	facts
share	kind of on the wild side	solve the problem	detail
work together	just take a sec'	bottom line	think about
smooth out the rough edges	chill out	reach the goal	consider
collaborate	brainstorm	work	evaluate
build consensus	innovate	do it now	review
improve morale	create	profit	outline
teamwork	pick your brain		curious
family	it'll be painless		a surprise
let's talk about it			interesting
			research

Telling Accommodators that the PDA has a feature that will help them *be more organized* might encourage them to use it. An Optimist, however, doesn't perceive the value of being organized. To Optimists, the key benefit is that using the feature that helps them to be more organized will *give them more free time*. To Producers, telling them this feature will help them *get more done* is meaningful. What might motivate a Data Collector is that this feature *keeps track of details*. One product, one feature, and four ways of expressing it.

In organizing the E-mail, remember to start with the benefit that's likely to motivate the Producers. For instance, you might say:

Get more done with less pain! Using your PDA helps you be more organized, which gives you more free time. All while keeping track of key details.

Notice we start with a direct statement targeting Producers (get more done). We then address Accommodators (be more organized), Optimists (enjoy free time), and Data Collectors (track details). This strategic approach is likely to help you achieve your objectives; by using the words and phrases that are meaningful to other people, in a sense what you're doing is speaking their language.

EXERCISE 2: *Target Your Reader's Personality*

Let's say that your favorite boss has asked you to write her a letter of reference. She is up for a "plum of a job" and is proactively gathering references. You're being asked to submit a letter as someone who knows her style and abilities as a boss. Your boss has asked that you write to the person she is interviewing with, Frank Smith.

Think about your favorite boss. It could be the person you worked for when you were in school, baby-sat, or mowed lawns. It could be your current boss. Whoever you chose, think about what sort of job this person would likely be applying for now. Think about what sort of person Mr. Smith is likely to be. You can't know, of course, but you can come up with an educated guess based on the job and environment Mr. Smith is in. You don't need to know what's in Mr. Smith's heart, nor do you need to know his essence. All you need to consider is what he is likely to value.

Turn back to the four personality types on page 7 and think about which one most likely describes Mr. Smith. Review Table 1.1 to get some words and phrases in your mind, then answer the questions below. After you've completed the exercise, read the comments that follow.

1. Write a one-sentence statement of your objective. Think action: What do you want Mr. Smith to do as a result of reading your letter?
2. What job is your favorite boss applying for?
3. What's Mr. Smith's personality type likely to be?
4. List a few qualities that make your boss stand out as a successful supervisor. (Note these are features.) For example, perhaps your boss has great technical knowledge, or perhaps she is able to give directions clearly.
5. For each quality (i.e., feature) use Table 1.1 to help you select a word or two to convert it into a benefit likely to appeal to Mr. Smith, based on his personality.

For example, if your boss has great technical knowledge and you determine that Mr. Smith is a Producer, you might convert the feature "great technical knowledge" into a benefit by expressing it as "Bottom line—she knows her stuff." If you determine that Mr. Smith is an Accommodator, however, you might express "great technical knowledge" as "reliable and solid technical know-how."

For "gives directions clearly," if you determine that Mr. Smith is an Optimist, you might express it as "she expresses herself well and is easy to understand." If you think that Mr. Smith is a Data Collector, you might translate "gives directions clearly" to "provides comprehensive, step-by-step instructions."

CREATE THE RIGHT IMAGE

Now that you understand the importance of setting an action-oriented objective, and you are able to identify benefits likely to target various personality types, you're ready to evaluate the appropriate level of formality.

Using the Formality Index, you'll answer three simple questions to determine how formal or informal your communication should be. This process helps select the format (e.g., E-mail vs. letter), the tone (e.g., Dear Mr. Jones vs. Dear Richard), and the style (e.g., chief executive officer vs. CEO).

We're an informal society becoming less formal all the time. The decision you make about what level of formality is best will help you create the mood you want. The level of formality sets the tone, creates an image, and has the potential to enhance your relationship with your readers.

The Formality Index asks you to answer three questions on a scale of one to ten, one meaning absolutely not or never and ten meaning absolutely yes or always. If you're uncertain, or if the answer is maybe, sort of, sometimes, or kind of, you would select a score of perhaps four, five, six, or seven. In other words, the higher your score, the closer you are to an absolute yes.

Here are the three questions:

1. Do you know your target reader(s) well and personally?
2. Are they below you in "rank"?
3. Is the subject of your communication good news?

Think about the first question. In business, you may never socialize with someone and yet feel as if you know them well and personally. For example, the coworker in the next cubicle with whom you've shared a cordial relationship for four years or the person you've bought office supplies from for two years might be in this category. The better you know someone, the higher your score.

The second question requires that you define what "rank" means to you. It doesn't refer to a formal system (like in the military). Rather it asks that you evaluate what, in your world, is held in high esteem. Some people value celebrity, age, education, status, accomplishment, job titles, and so on. The more you perceive that you're above your readers (using whatever standards you select), the higher your score.

The third question asks you to consider how the people you're writing to are likely to perceive the content of your message. As you evaluate whether you're delivering good news or not, remember that you can't fake it; just because you think your company's new product is terrific doesn't mean the people you're advertising it to will agree. Are you announcing a raise? That's a ten! Layoffs? That's a one.

Notice that all three questions require that you make judgments. There's no right or wrong, but there are real differences. Consider this example: Let's say that you're sending a tin of chocolate chip cookies to your son who's away at college. You're sending the cookies with a "good luck on your finals and I love you" message.

1. *Do you know your target reader(s) well and personally?*
   Yes. You score it a ten.
2. *Are they below you in "rank"?*
   Some people say, "Yes, you bet he's below me in 'rank'!" If that's your feeling, you'd score it a ten. Others say, "No, we're equals," and score it a one.
3. *Is the subject of your communication good news?*
   Yes! You're sending cookies—it's a ten.

Your total score is likely to be somewhere between twenty and thirty. The higher the score, the less formal the communication should be. Doesn't it make sense in this case that the note you'll include with the cookies should be quite informal? Now answer the questions while considering a different situation.

Let's say you want to apply for a job. You've found a posting on a website that seems perfect. The ad instructs you to send your résumé and a cover letter.

1. *Do you know your target reader(s) well and personally?*
   No. You've never met the person you're writing to. You score it a one.
2. *Are they below you in "rank"?*
   Most of us would consider a person who has the power to hire us for a job we've defined as "ideal" as above us in "rank" and would therefore assess it as a one. But let us assume that you are at a very high level yourself and that the person you're writing to is only slightly above you or is your equal. Even under these circumstances, the most you are likely to score this question is a five or a six.
3. *Is the subject of your communication good news?*
   It's tempting to think "Yes!—I'm perfect for the job"—score this a ten! Avoid puffery. Certainly it makes sense that your score will be rather high—otherwise why would you apply for the job. But in considering the proper level of formality—the format,

tone, and style that's best—it's important to assess whether your communication is "good news" objectively, that is, from your reader's point of view. At the same time, you don't want to diminish yourself. If modesty leads you to conclude that a fair score is a one, ask yourself why you are applying for the job. In this case, let's say that you truly believe you're a strong candidate for the job. You score this question an eight.

Your total score will range from a low of three to a high of thirty. The lower the score, the more formal the communication should be. In this example, your total score is ten $(1 + 1 + 8 = 10)$. A score of ten implies that your communication should be quite formal. With few exceptions, most of us would agree that letters of application for jobs are among the most formal communications we produce. Once you know what level of formality is most suitable for your communication to your target reader, you're in a good position to make the following three decisions:

1. format
2. style
3. tone

Format

The most formal communication format is the one that's been around the longest: a standard letter on conventional letterhead. The least formal business communication is E-mail. Think about this: No matter how serious your message, no matter how little you know someone, and no matter to whom you're writing, if you send your communication via E-mail, it will be perceived as less formal than if it's on paper. That doesn't mean you should not send important communications via E-mail. It does imply that critical, sober messages that are sent via E-mail should use a formal tone and style to compensate for the informal medium.

Here are the least formal media formats:

- flyers
- newsletters

- handwritten notes
- margin notes
- sticky notes
- E-mails

Here are the most formal media formats:

- letters on letterhead
- proposals
- legal documents
- brochures
- E-mail attachments, if formally constructed

Style

The following lists provide guidelines for creating formal, standard, or informal communications.

To maintain the most formal style, be sure to:

- Refer to people by their last names, using the honorifics Mr., Ms., or Dr. (Note that "Ms." is now considered the standard honorific when addressing a woman in business.)
- Avoid acronyms; spell out terms every time they are used.
- Adhere to academic standards (don't begin sentences with "but," "because," "and," or "so," for instance).
- Use large margins.
- Close your communication with either "Sincerely" or "Yours truly."
- Sign both your first and last names.
- Assume no previous knowledge on your reader's part (use appendices or attachments to clarify or summarize details).

To maintain a standard business style (neither formal nor informal), be sure to:

- Refer to people by their last names until you've met or spoken to them, and then use their first names.

- Only use an acronym after you've written out the term it represents completely the first time you use it, followed by the acronym within parentheses; you then can use the acronym throughout the rest of the document. For example, the first time you would write:

  English as a Foreign Language (EFL)

  Thereafter, you would use EFL.
- Model sentence structure on business conversation; thus, you may begin sentences with "but," "because," "and," or "so," for example.
- Use standard margins.
- Close your communication with "Regards," "Yours," or another favorite business term.
- Sign or type your first name.
- Assume prior knowledge (if it exists).

To maintain the most informal style, be sure to:

- Refer to people by their first names.
- Use acronyms.
- Use relaxed sentence structures, such as phrases instead of sentences, and frequently begin sentences with words such as "but," "because," "and," or "so."
- Avoid letterhead; instead, use memo pads, sticky notes, or send your message via E-mail.
- Close with your first name or initials (even in E-mail).
- Assume a great deal of prior knowledge; abbreviations, acronyms, and references to inside information are common.
- Maintain a proper business-like look and feel.

Tone

Tone refers to the overall feeling conveyed by your writing. Beyond individual writing styles, there are techniques you can use to sound no-nonsense, rational, friendly, or urgent. Formal communications tend to be no-nonsense or rational. Informal communications tend to be friendly or urgent.

Use the following as a guide as you begin the writing process:

- To sound *no-nonsense*, use the imperative, i.e., begin sentences with verbs. When you begin sentences with verbs, you encourage action. For example, "Attend the meeting," "Fill out the form," or "Return the phone call."
- To sound *rational*, use a logical progression. For instance, "First you turn on the computer, then you insert the CD into drive D, then you . . . "
- To sound *friendly*, create empathy with words and phrases that suggest a specific mood or atmosphere likely to strike a chord with your reader. For example, instead of "ABC Bank is pleased to announce that it will sponsor a jazz concert every Friday at seven throughout the summer," say "Picture yourself relaxing at the evening jazz concerts sponsored by ABC Bank every Friday at seven throughout the summer."
- Also, use a conversational tone, as if you were there in person. For instance, instead of "Per our agreement . . . ," say "As we agreed . . . "
- To sound *urgent*, stress deadlines or consequences. For example, instead of "Please return the form at your earliest convenience," say "Please return the form by Tuesday, August 21."

A Standard Business Document

A *standard* communication is achieved through a combination of elements. For example, you may use a conversational style in a traditional letter.

If you decide that it's appropriate to create a *formal* communication:

1. You should use a traditional format (such as a report, proposal, or letter).
2. Your style should be conventional.
3. Your tone should be no-nonsense, rational, or urgent.

If you decide that it's appropriate to create an *informal* communication:

1. You should use a nontraditional format (such as E-mail, a margin note, or a sticky note).
2. Your style should be relaxed and personalized.
3. Your tone should be friendly.

Consider the communications in Figures 1.1 and 1.2. One is formal, the other is standard, or less formal. Both address a typical business situation: The letter writer is requesting a partial refund for inadequate service.

In Figure 1.1, you'll note a rather formal tone. (The Formality Index was judged as $1 + 5 + 1 = 7$.)

Now consider that the writer assesses the Formality Index as standard—not informal, but certainly more relaxed than the formal letter. (It is scored as $7 + 8 + 3 = 18$.)

EXERCISE 3: *How Formal Should Your Communication Be?*

If you use the Formality Index to assess how your communication should be formatted and how it should sound, your readers will be more likely to respond as you intend. Think about the project you worked on earlier—writing a letter of reference to Mr. Smith on behalf of your favorite boss.

Answer the three questions in the Formality Index to determine the appropriate level of formality:

1. Do you know your target reader(s) well and personally?
2. Are they below you in "rank"?
3. Is the subject of your communication good news?

What did you decide? Most people evaluate this communication as one that's quite formal—did you? (Most people would score this between ten and twenty; for example, $1 + 2 + 9 = 12$.)

Once you complete the Formality Index, you're ready to move on to the final tool of this chapter. This third tool, the Matrix of Persuasion, helps you classify your overall writing assignment. Doing so enables you to understand, strategically, how best to present benefits to your target readers.

Acme Widgets and Frammis Joints
1212 Fourteenth Street
Des Plaines, Illinois 86726
Telephone: 212.555.1212   Fax: 212.555.1212

Date

Mr. Wilson's name,
title, and
company address

Dear Mr. Wilson:

Your company has been one of our vendors
for several years. Each year we purchase a
maintenance contract. On September 8 of this
year, we called for service. If you would kindly
review the attached log, you'll see that we had
to place four calls before we received a call-
back, and it was two full days before a technician arrived.

This level of responsiveness is unacceptable
to us and is below your stated guarantee;
therefore, I am writing to request a partial
refund of our maintenance contract. It seems
to me that a refund of one month's fee would
be fair. Please ensure that a check for that
amount is sent directly to our accounts
payable department.

Sincerely,
Your name and title here

Figure 1.1 A Formal Letter on Letterhead

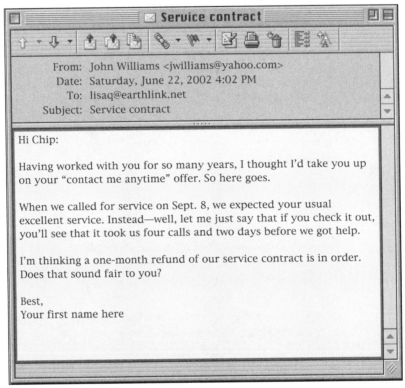

Figure 1.2 An Informal E-mail

BIG PICTURE:
USE THE MATRIX OF PERSUASION

We've focused on you and your needs (your objective) and your readers and their needs (those benefits that are likely to motivate them). We've considered the proper level of formality—a time-saver if you consider it early on in the writing process. Now it's time to pull your thinking together by pausing for a moment and considering the big picture. The Matrix of Persuasion allows you to analyze your overall writing assignment.

In the Matrix of Persuasion, two variables are contrasted: Is your target audience on your side or not on your side; and do your readers have the requisite resources or are they constrained? (See Exhibit 1.1.)

	On Your Side	**Not on Your Side**
No or Few Constraints	Easy • facts only • short copy okay	Persuade or Educate • benefits matter • longer copy needed
Constraints	Problem-solve • Q&A • longer copy needed	Hard • rarely worthwhile

Exhibit 1.1 Matrix of Persuasion

By identifying which of the four quadrants your writing task fits into, you'll be better able to identify your readers' needs, and thus write more focused first drafts in less time.

As you review the matrix in Exhibit 1.1, note that you're first asked to determine if your target readers are "on your side" or "not on your side." Think about the people you're trying to reach. Do they know you? Do they like you? Are they predisposed in your favor? Or are they not?

Next, consider whether they're capable of doing what you ask or are constrained. Do they have the requisite time, authority, interest, motivation, money, or whatever resources are needed to do what you're hoping they will do? Or are there constraints that you'll need to help them overcome?

Let's say, for example, that your boss asks you to investigate venues for the company's annual Christmas party. You're given a budget of $1,000 and told to make a recommendation. You find the perfect place. It's close to work, it's got a diverse menu, and the price quoted is less than your $1,000 budget.

Wouldn't you agree that your boss is "on your side"? And there are no constraints. In other words, this is an *Easy* writing assignment. As the matrix indicates, this means you can send a one- or two-line message simply stating the facts.

But what if you find a venue that's perfect except it costs $1,200? Your boss is still "on your side." But there's a constraint. You don't have the money in your budget. Therefore, in order to achieve your objective, it's important that you *Problem-solve*. You might E-mail your boss, for

Let's say, for example, that your boss asks you to investigate venues for the company's annual Christmas party. You're given a budget of $1,000 and told to make a recommendation. You find the perfect place. It's close to work, it's got a diverse menu, and the price quoted is less than your $1,000 budget.

Wouldn't you agree that your boss is "on your side"? And there are no constraints. In other words, this is an *Easy* writing assignment. As the matrix indicates, this means you can send a one-or two-line message simply stating the facts.

But what if you find a venue that's perfect except it costs $1,200? Your boss is still "on your side." But there's a constraint. You don't have the money in your budget. Therefore, in order to achieve your objective, it's important that you *Problem-solve*. You might E-mail your boss, for example, and tell her that you'll commit to planning a summer picnic that's $200 under budget if you can go $200 over budget now.

Now let's say you decide that rather than a conventional Christmas party you want to recommend something different: that the company pay for all employees to go to a Christmas concert sponsored by a local chamber music group. The price of the tickets would be within your budget. Doesn't it make sense that you need to *Persuade or Educate* your boss? There are no constraints in terms of money or time, but there is some question as to whether your boss will think attending a concert is a good idea. As the matrix indicates, you need to focus on benefits, and more than one communication may be required for you to succeed.

You might also consider using a Q&A format. A Q&A format allows you to anticipate your readers' questions and answer them. Because you pose the questions, you can be certain to word them in a positive way (by talking about benefits or how to avoid negative outcomes), and you're able to control the flow of information.

Now let's say that the concert tickets will total $5,000, but you love the idea, so you decide to proceed with recommending the concert. Your boss is "not on your side," and you are constrained—you're way over budget. This is *Hard*. To succeed, you need to both persuade your boss and problem-solve.

Sometimes you go forward with Hard communications, even though you think your chances of success are slim, for legal reasons, or because you feel strongly about an issue.

For example, suppose your insurance company refuses to settle on a property damage claim after a hurricane, citing the fact that you didn't have hurricane insurance. You feel that it's an issue of poor construction, not weather—specifically, you believe that if the building wall had been built properly, it wouldn't have fallen in the rain. You therefore decide to write a letter of protest to the president of the insurance company. They have precedent, policy, and the law on their side; your indignation, however, transcends mere law, and it makes you feel better to write a good, stiff letter of protest.

EXERCISE 4: *Put the Matrix of Persuasion to Work*

Use the matrix to evaluate the project that has you writing to Mr. Smith about your favorite boss. Which quadrant do you think the project is in? Is Mr. Smith "on your side" or "not on your side"? Is Mr. Smith constrained against doing what you support?

If you decided that you need to Persuade and Educate, that gives you important information. (About 80 percent of all written business communications are in the Persuade and Educate quadrant. Those goals—to persuade and educate—are common business activities.) As you continue developing the letter, doesn't it make sense that you're going to want to include several benefit statements? Given that you'll need to prove each benefit's value to Mr. Smith's company, isn't it likely that the letter will be long rather than short, and that you may ask Mr. Smith to contact you for additional information?

Perhaps you consider the letter to Mr. Smith Easy. If Mr. Smith is predisposed to hire an excellent candidate—in your view, your favorite boss—and if there's a job available, you may be right. If you are, you may want to keep your letter short and factual.

If your favorite boss is trying for a career change, perhaps this is a Problem-solving communication, and you should organize your message to demonstrate how your boss's experience translates into the new job's requirements.

Almost by definition, you wouldn't be writing a reference letter that's Hard—but, of course, it's possible. (If your favorite boss is trying for a job for which he or she is in no way qualified, then it would certainly be a Hard letter.)

The Matrix of Persuasion is a "big picture" tool. It helps you get your thoughts in order. It allows you to take what you know—your objective, your target readers, and the proper level of formality—and consider how best to use this information to reach your target readers.

In the next chapter, we're going to review nine organizational structures and begin to put pen to paper or fingers to keyboard—and write.

CHAPTER TWO

Create a Draft on Paper (or on Your Computer)

GOOD WRITING STARTS WITH CLEAR THINKING

In the last chapter, we discussed the importance of using a methodical process in writing. You learned to set objectives, analyze your audience, and determine how formal a tone you should adopt. In this chapter, we're going to compare and contrast nine organizational structures, consider visual writing techniques, review traditional outlining, and discuss an alternative to traditional outlining called Hub & Spokes.

CHOOSE YOUR ORGANIZATIONAL STRUCTURE

Selecting an organizational structure before you begin to write makes the actual writing process easier and more straightforward. If you recognize that you have several separate issues that need to be addressed, you might decide to use the category structure. Having made that decision, the next step is clear: identify your categories.

On the other hand, if you decide to write using a chronology structure, you won't list categories; instead, you'll start at the beginning and continue on sequentially.

As you review the nine organizational structures on the next page, consider the versatility and limitations of each, and note that no one organizational structure is better than another. The sections that follow are intended to help you understand how to make a decision about which organizational structure is appropriate for your project.

It's important to keep in mind that any project can use a combination of organizational structures. For example, consider an operating guide on how to use a washing machine. The guide might use a combination of the chronology and category organizational structures. The overall structure might be categorical (i.e., *Before You Begin, Regular Washing Cycle, Delicate Cycle, Troubleshooting Guide*, and so on). Within each category, however, the detailed instructions are likely to be organized chronologically (e.g., the *Before You Begin* section might start with "Before using your new washing machine, read the following safety instructions.").

Certain categories might use several structures. For instance, the *Troubleshooting Guide* (category) might list subcategories (i.e., machine won't spin). Within each subcategory, perhaps the guide would use a PAR (problem/action/results) approach combined with a chronological approach (e.g., "First see if the 'unbalanced' light is illuminated.").

Sometimes it's best to organize your content using a visual layout, such as a matrix or bulleted points.

There are a multitude of combinations. And there's no right or wrong approach. Make your choice based on the kind of project you're working on and what information you want to highlight.

The nine organizational structures are:

1. chronology
2. category
3. PAR (problem [or opportunity]/action/results)
4. Q&A
5. visual layout

. . . plus four ways to say no or deliver bad news:

6. Bookend No
7. No with an Alternative
8. Diplomatic No
9. Direct No

It's important to understand each organizational structure's strengths and when to use each one. Each of the nine structures suggests a framework. Once you begin to work with the structures, you'll see how adhering to the standards streamlines and simplifies the entire writing process.

Chronology: Highlight the Evolution of Events

The chronology organizational structure lays out the sequence of a set of events. Instruction manuals and updates are common applications of this structure.

Instruction Manuals

A training manual might use the chronology structure to describe the steps involved in installing a new software program by saying, "First, put the CD in the D drive and slide the drawer closed. Second, click on the 'Start' icon. Third, click on the word 'Program,'" and so on.

Mark, a corporate trainer for an automobile repair firm, explained it this way: "I discovered early on that you can't oversimplify instruction manuals. By using the chronology organizational structure, I make sure I don't skip any steps."

Updates

An update or status report frequently summarizes past events to put current information in context.

"I prepared an update for my boss about our efforts to resolve some manufacturing issues," Aaron, manager at a pharmaceutical company who is responsible for quality control, explained. "I began the report by saying, 'Last May I met with my counterpart at ABC Corporation, and we identified several quality control issues. We agreed to address the issues by creating and empowering a team. The team, comprising three customer engineers and three of our staff members, met for the first time in June. Thereafter, this team met once a month and issued their recommendations in November. (See Appendix A.)'

"Using the chronology organizational structure allowed me to highlight the scope of the initiative. Our recommendations weren't made on a whim—we spent a lot of time thinking first. Only by starting at the beginning would this evolution be clear."

Category: Focus on the Scope of Events

The category organizational structure helps break large projects into manageable units; for this reason, this structure is frequently used in proposals and reports. The category organizational structure is also appropriate for matter-of-fact short narratives, such as announcements and E-mails.

Proposals

Proposals typically use a category organizational structure to make it easy for readers to locate specific units of information.

Michelle, for instance, wrote a grant request that ran more than fifty pages. "It was a huge endeavor. The museum that I work for wanted to install new lighting, and I wrote a proposal to a private foundation that provides funds for infrastructure improvements. I chose the category organizational structure as a way of making the huge amount of information manageable.

"I ended up with six categories:

1. our attendance figures
2. testimonials from curators about the importance of lighting
3. an engineering report about fine art lighting standards
4. an electrician's cost estimates
5. background information about the museum and how we serve the community
6. copies of legal documents proving our nonprofit status

"As I wrote the proposal, I kept discovering new categories. Having selected the category organizational structure, I was able to easily add new categories, combine some closely related ones, and eliminate some that weren't relevant. I can't imagine how much more difficult it would have been if I had been trying to track and revise one fifty-page unit instead of the smaller, easy-to-identify units.

"We got the money, by the way!"

Reports

The category organizational structure also works well in reports. Using this structure ensures that each section is short and focused, two standards of excellence in business writing.

Karl's boss expected each of his direct subordinates to write a monthly activity report. Karl explained that he used to use a straight narrative format. "It was sort of chronological in that I used my calendar to help me remember what I did, but it was a mishmash. On the third of the month, for example, I might have reviewed the closing financials of the month before. That would tickle my memory that I worked on next year's capital budget during the last week of the month, and so I'd digress about that. The activity report was disorganized and hard to follow.

"Once I started using the category organizational structure, the entire process became more manageable. As a financial analyst, my work is pretty routine. So I was able to set categories and then simply update the report each month. It saved me hours of work. And the report was easier to read and more focused."

Announcements

Simple announcements (of, say, a new product introduction or a promotion) often use a category organizational structure to highlight certain elements.

Thomas explained, "In the announcement of Dawn's promotion, I wanted to focus on her ability to bring people together. I structured the memo—which I sent as an E-mail attachment to all employees, the press, and key customers—using phrases that stressed her diplomatic skills as subheadings. Rather than simply list disciplines like supervisory and financial, for instance, I stressed the different aspects of her ability as a diplomat. The categories I included, and used as subheadings, were 'bridging differences,' 'forging alliances,' and 'building relationships.' Once I identified the categories, the announcement wrote itself."

E-mails

Given that E-mails are usually shorter than other forms of communication, they usually feature only one category of content. Longer E-mails, however, can be divided into content categories.

Julie Ann explained that as a purchasing agent for an industrial belting company, she communicates with vendors via E-mail all the time. "What I've found most effective is listing my questions and asking that they respond to them one by one. In other words, *I* set the categories for *their* responses."

PAR (Problem [or Opportunity]/Action/Results): Get to the Bottom Line

When the outcome is the most significant part of your message, the PAR organizational structure is the form to use to highlight your results. PAR is an effective organizational structure in résumés and sales letters.

Résumés

By focusing on your bottom-line accomplishments, i.e., the impact your actions had on your employer, you help your reader see why employing you is in his or her best interest.

Marianne wanted a new job. "When I began the process of looking for a new job, I was completely frustrated. My company was in terrible shape. We'd been downsized to within an inch of our lives, we were all doing the jobs that used to be done by two, even three people, and I was fed up. But I recognized that my frustration was of no interest to potential employers. What I did was focus on my accomplishments, and I stated them in the context of solving problems or taking advantage of opportunities.

"For example, instead of 'responsible for supervising three outside gardening staff,' I wrote, 'reduced replacement shrubbery cost by 11 percent by adjusting the schedule of three outside gardeners to provide better coverage.'

"The bottom line is that I got a great new job!"

Q&A: Position News and Information

Using a Q&A organizational structure allows you to control how news and information will be perceived. Word questions so that they stress a benefit or highlight how to avoid a negative outcome. It's an effective approach in newsletter articles and procedure manuals.

Newsletter Articles

It's not uncommon to have to publish bad news in a newsletter. Don explained that he's the newsletter editor for a chemical distributor. "Last month, for instance, I had to write an article telling the independent distributors who are part of our consortium that if they cross a state line, they're liable for damages under new federal statutes. It's important that they know this information. But I also know human nature. If I ran an article about a new law that increases their exposure, they'd toss the newsletter aside—not because they don't want to know, but because they'd hope to avoid it a little bit longer.

"So what I did was position the information in a positive way. I used a headline that read 'Five Strategies You Can Use Now.' The introductory paragraph read 'The five strategies detailed below can help protect you from liability. It's under your control.' Then I began with a Q&A. Instead of asking 'Do you want to know your liability?' I phrased it as 'What can I do to avoid liability?' Every question was worded as a positive or neutral statement."

Procedure Manuals

Procedure manuals often force employees to read through long-winded narratives filled with legalese. Consider using a Q&A organizational structure instead.

Amy, director of computer services for an entertainment conglomerate, said, "I organized the entire procedure manual using a category organizational structure. Within each category, I used a Q&A organizational structure. It worked well. In fact, it was so effective that, during a recent revision, I added an index that listed all the questions covered in the manual by category.

"I made sure that all the questions were positive. I wanted to highlight certain policies, and I positioned those questions first. For example, in the section that detailed our policy against sending jokes or cartoons, I wanted to highlight that our concern is to protect against viruses, not to stifle humor or imply that cartoons are a waste of time. After all, we're an entertainment company. Instead of 'Why can't I send jokes or cartoons via E-mail?' I phrased it as 'How can I help protect the company against viruses?'"

Note how important it is to choose words carefully. Simply avoiding a negative word ("can't") and using positive words ("help protect") conveys an upbeat message.

Visual Layout: Ensure Easy Access to Information

Using a visual layout makes sense when you have long units of copy containing more than five facts, statistics, or numbers. For example, consider an annual report that asks readers to compare the past four quarters' revenue figures within a paragraph of text. No problem. But now imagine being asked to compare the past twelve months' revenue figures within a paragraph of text. Impossible.

Instead of narrative text, use a bar chart to make the information easy to access and easy to understand. The visual layout organizational structure is effective anytime you have a quantity of data that needs to be accessible. The information can be presented as a graph, chart, table, diagram, schematic, matrix, list, or bulleted points. You can use a visual layout in addition to or instead of narrative text. Employee benefits booklets and proposals are examples of materials for which a visual layout organizational structure works well.

Employee Benefits Booklets

Consider how easy it would be to locate the information you seek using Table 2.1. If you're a full-time employee wanting to compare your benefits to those of part-time employees, you can simply scan the columns and note the differences.

Proposals

"I combined a visual layout organizational structure with a category organizational structure," said Chad, an engineer. "Our proposals have to reach two different kinds of people: Data Collectors, who have a technical background and want a lot of technical details; and Producers, who don't want the details but instead want a summary, bottom-line overview.

"Using this format made a huge difference. We won more contracts—and nothing had changed except the addition of the visual layout organizational structure.

"I've always used a category organizational structure. Now, on every page of the proposal I create an 'Executive Summary' in a narrow column. I use a bullet point to highlight an important benefit or a key statistic, for example. The wider column is regular text." (See Exhibit 2.1.)

This approach, segregating different kinds of content to target different groups of readers or to highlight different kinds of information, is a versatile strategy.

Table 2.1 Full-Time vs. Part-Time Employee Benefits

	Full-Time Employees	Part-Time Employees
Vacation	× weeks after 1 year's service	× hours after 1 year's service
	× weeks after 5 years' service	× hours after 5 years' service
	× weeks after 8 years' service	× hours after 8 years' service
Health Insurance	× percent company paid	× percent company paid
Sick Days	× paid days per year	× paid days per year, prorated
Holidays	× days per year	× days per year
Professional Development	Paid as agreed upon between employees and their supervisors	Paid as agreed upon between employees and their supervisors, prorated

Bookend No: Convey Goodwill

Using the Bookend No organizational structure allows you to make bad news palatable. It won't convert bad news into good news, nor will it make the recipient happy, but it is the best way to convey negative information.

The Bookend No organizational structure starts with a positive statement, leads into the negative news, and finishes with another positive statement. Note that you can't fake it, i.e., if you have nothing positive to say, you can't use this organizational structure. It works well with letters and informal E-mails.

Executive Summary	Begin Each Section with a Heading
• A statistic or key benefit here.	Text running in the wider column using traditional paragraphs and headings allows for two different kinds of access: scanning and reading. When the narrative text relates to the Executive Summary on the same page, it's easy for a reader who is simply scanning the summary to read text that is of interest and skip or skim the rest.
• Another short point here.	
• A compelling testimonial here that may run for several lines but looks shorter because it's positioned in a narrow sidebar.	**A Subheading Here Breaks Up the Text**
	Readers who are interested in the details will be able to get the information they seek by reading the text positioned in the wider column. Your text can run for as many pages as needed.
	You should aim to have about the same number of bulleted points on each page, just as you should try to have roughly the same quantity of text on each page.
• Another key benefit here. The text about the benefit may run several lines.	**Another Heading Indicates a New Section**
	The narrative continues on from one page to the next as it would in a traditional one-column proposal. This layout allows readers to read just the information they choose.

Exhibit 2.1 A Dual-Purpose Layout

Letters

Sonya needed to write letters to people who had interviewed for a job and weren't going to be offered the position. "In many cases," she explained, "the applicants were very nice people. They just weren't the best. I created a letter that served this purpose beautifully. Here it is."

Date

Name and address of recipient

Dear name of recipient:

Thank you for taking the time to meet with us regarding the xyz position. We were impressed with your background and experience.

However, we are unable to offer you a position at this time.

With your impressive credentials, I'm certain that you'll find the perfect job soon. I wish you much success in your endeavors.

Sincerely,
My name and signature here

"I was aware that no one receiving the letter would like getting it—after all, I'm telling them that they didn't get the job. But I think it's worded in as positive a way as possible." Note that the bad news is "book-ended" by paragraphs of not bad (thanks for interviewing) or positive (reference to good credentials) remarks.

Informal E-Mails

When Martin got an E-mail from a new employee suggesting a media buy they'd tried a few months before the employee had joined the company, he didn't hesitate to use the Bookend No organizational structure. "I wanted to reward her initiative. At the same time, I had to shoot down her idea. The Bookend No organizational structure allowed me to do both. I E-mailed her 'Thanks for the idea, but we tried it without success just a few months ago. (See the file on xyz.) I'm impressed with your initiative. Keep those ideas coming; the more the better!'"

No with an Alternative: Share Ideas

Sometimes, even though you need to say no to something, you might have an idea that would be of value to your readers. The No with an Alternative organizational structure is appropriate when you have a viable alternative to suggest. It might be used on a website or in a letter.

Website

Fran said that she used the No with an Alternative organizational structure on her website. "When we decided to stop producing a certain brand of shampoo, we knew there'd be some disappointed customers. But it was a done deal—we were closing down the product line. It wasn't profitable and, strategically, we wanted to move in other directions. My job was to announce the decision in such a way that we didn't alienate customers. After all, they might be buying soap and other products from us in addition to the shampoo.

"I added a page on our website to explain our strategic shift and suggest alternative products. It was the *Miracle on 34th Street* Macy's sending them to Gimble's idea. I positioned it with my boss by explaining that it provided extraordinary customer service. I was a little nervous, but I can't tell you how well it worked. We got hundreds—literally hundreds—of thank you messages, all because I offered a viable alternative."

Letters

Sonya, who created the rejection letter using the Bookend No organizational structure (see page 35), explained, "The candidate I'd selected was amazing. My boss concurred. Bob was the nicest fellow, and so well qualified. But just as I'm about to pick up the phone and offer Bob the job, guess what? My boss tells me that a corporate-wide hiring freeze has just been announced. So instead of hiring Bob, I had to write him a letter telling him I couldn't hire him. I called my husband for some sympathy, and he told me that his colleague Leo was looking for someone just like Bob.

"That was great. Instead of a letter using the Bookend No organizational structure, I was able to write a letter using the No with an Alternative organizational structure."

Date

Bob's name and address

Dear Bob:

Given that you are the perfect candidate for the xyz position, I am very disappointed to have to report that we have just instituted a hiring freeze. I don't know how long it's going to last; thus, I am unable to offer you the job.

However, I understand that Leo (last name) at ABC Corporation is looking for someone with your background and experience. It might be a perfect opportunity for you. Good luck!

I do hope you'll stay in touch. Perhaps we'll be able to work together at some point in the future.

Sincerely,
My name and signature here

"The letter wrote itself once I selected the organizational structure."

Diplomatic No: Avoid Confrontations

When you need to say no but want to either retain the relationship or, at the very least, avoid alienating your readers, consider the Diplomatic No. By focusing on the process by which the decision to say no was derived, you avoid saying anything personal. Form letters and press releases are often written using the Diplomatic No organizational structure.

Form Letters

Sonya (see above) said that she talked to more than two dozen candidates during the hiring process. She decided to send a form letter to a dozen or so—those candidates she'd spoken to on the telephone but hadn't interviewed.

"I had nothing particularly against them but nothing nice to say either. I wanted to be respectful in telling them they weren't going to get the job. The Diplomatic No organizational structure served the purpose perfectly. I started with 'Dear Applicant' because I wanted the tone to be impersonal."

Date

Dear Applicant:

In the course of filling the xyz position, we reviewed scores of applicants' credentials. The process was long, and one we took very seriously. Often candidates with impressive credentials are not suitable for one of several reasons, including a lack of relevant experience or inadequate job knowledge, for example.

Although I'm unable to offer you a job at this time, I want to thank you for taking the time to apply for the position.

Sincerely,
My name here

"The thing I liked was that it wouldn't hurt them, even though it conveyed bad news," Sonya said.

Note that Sonya wrote nothing personal. The entire focus was on the process of selecting a candidate; no part of the letter mentioned anything individual or specific. While the unsuccessful applicants won't like getting the letter, neither will it sting.

Press Releases

Major corporations frequently use the Diplomatic No organizational structure when they need to announce bad news to the public. The strategy works whether the announcement is made via E-mail, a newsletter, a memo, or a press release.

A press release is an announcement of a newsworthy event issued to the media. To have the best chance of having your press release published, it needs to be more than relevant—it needs to be written concisely. The less revision a publication has to do, the more likely the release is to be published.

Many organizations use press releases to announce events, performances, mergers and acquisitions, promotions, and other positive business developments. They can also be used effectively to announce bad news. Jim, CEO of an auto parts manufacturer, used a press release to announce a downturn in sales, for example.

"I met with all employees in person, of course. But using a press release allowed us to control how the news was positioned to the public. I used the Diplomatic No organizational structure and it worked well. Don't get me wrong: Bad news is bad news, but it could have been much worse if our stockholders, vendors, and customers heard rumors before we'd made the announcement."

The introductory sentence in Jim's press release was in the third person and used the passive voice, usually a style to be avoided. But in this case it resulted in a rational, calm tone that was necessary to avoid rumors. It began:

> ABC corporation announced today that third-quarter sales were projected to be 8 percent lower than previously expected. Jim (last name here), CEO, said, "Most companies involved in the automobile industry are experiencing a downturn. As a parts manufacturer, we're at the front of the curve. We're looking forward to an economic upswing, perhaps as early as the fourth quarter, and in the meantime, we're optimistic about our plans for global expansion.

Direct No: Protect Yourself

When asked to do something illegal, unethical, or immoral, it's important to be clear and unequivocal in saying no. The Direct No organizational structure is the most appropriate approach. Kya, a high school guidance counselor, explained that one morning she walked into her office to be greeted by a fax from an overseas contact.

"I'd met him during a holiday trip some years earlier. His business was helping students of his country apply to American colleges and universities. The fax said that one of his clients had been rejected from his first-choice university and despite calling, E-mailing, and faxing, they couldn't get anyone from the admissions department to tell them why he'd been rejected. Their idea was to find out why the student had been rejected and fix the problem.

"Given they had been unable to get any information, he was writing to me in the hope that I'd arrange for someone to break into the admissions department to find and photocopy the student's records. Can you imagine?"

Kya went on to explain that she'd considered ignoring the fax but decided she had to respond. "You never know where letters like that will end up ten years later," she said. "So I felt I needed to do something. But I didn't know what.

"Given that I wanted to say no, I knew I should consider the four organizational structures that specifically deal with delivering bad news.

"It seemed obvious that I didn't want to say anything positive, so the Bookend No wouldn't work. I can tell you that I didn't feel like saying 'Thanks so much for thinking of me.' The No with an Alternative wouldn't work either. What was I going to say? Go see Big Eddy on the corner? The Diplomatic No wouldn't help; I didn't want to preserve the relationship. Given that I'd decided I couldn't just do nothing, I felt I had no choice—I had to be direct.

"I ended up sending him a two-line response. I told him that I was stunned and appalled that he would suggest such a thing. No, I wouldn't break into the university admissions department."

Note that Kya used the organizational structures as a checklist. By methodically thinking how each one would sound, her choice became straightforward and easy to make.

"I'm pleased to report," Kya added, "that I never heard from him again."

EXERCISE 5: *Select an Organizational Structure*

For each of the following projects, select an appropriate organizational structure. Remember that there's no right answer. Think about your likely objective, what action you want your target readers to take as a result of reading your material, and how formal your writing should be. After making your choices, read how other people thought through their decisions.

1. Upon your return from a three-day industry conference, your boss asks you to write a "quick summary" of what you accomplished. What format do you choose and which organizational structure do you use?

2. You've been asked to inform senior managers about your depart-ment's progress in reaching a business objective. What organizational structure would you select?
3. You want to invite your team to your house for a social event. What organizational structure would you use?

1. Upon your return from a three-day industry conference, your boss asks you to write a "quick summary" of what you accomplished. What format do you choose and which organizational structure do you use?

Elinor, an Internet strategist at a cosmetics company, was expected to produce a report after she attended a conference called *Optimizing E-Commerce in the 21st Century*. "The instruction to write a report seemed very vague," she explained. "I wasn't sure exactly why I was sup-posed to write a report, so I asked my boss and she said that the report would let everybody know what I did while I was in Chicago and stress that it was a good idea that I'd gone.

"I decided that my objective should be to have top management request a full proposal based on my recommendation.

"Using this system helped me realize that I could use the report to cre-ate momentum for my own agenda. I'd do what my boss said—let peo-ple know why attending the conference was a good idea—and at the same time focus on my ideas for the company. I thought it would make me look like a go-getter, not a drone reporting on an activity in a passive way.

"Next I considered the senior managers' personalities. My boss and her boss are pretty technically oriented. They are both Data Collectors, with a little bit of Producer in the mix. The CEO, on the other hand, is mostly an Accommodator, with a little of both Optimist and Producer in her personality.

"I wanted to focus on an idea I had to use a digital camera that would allow women standing at a cosmetics counter to have their photo immedi-ately displayed on a monitor. They could see how different makeup options looked and make educated purchase decisions. We'd also E-mail the photo to them so they could play around with makeup options later—making deci-sions in the privacy of their own home or office, and on their own schedule.

"My strategy was to establish an E-mail relationship with our customers in a consultative way, and eventually convert their purchases to online transactions. What I was recommending was pretty aggressive strategi-cally because I wanted to offer customers the opportunity to delay buying our products. But I was convinced it would ultimately create long-term, committed customers. For instance, a customer could E-mail us that she wanted a new look for her daughter's wedding, and just when she's at her busiest and most frantic, we could respond with a personalized, specific recommendation, and not just with words, but by adjusting her photo to show her how she'd look with different makeup options."

Elinor consulted the vocabulary chart (see Table 1.1 on page 9) and said, "I looked for words and phrases that spoke to both a Data Collector and an Accommodator. Then I added some to speak to a Producer. It became clear to me that I should focus on the benefits to the company of helping our customers make decisions in a low-key, nonpressured way.

"When I consulted the Formality Index, I realized that I knew them well and personally—sort of. I'd been in the job a little over a year, and I got along well with everyone there. But it wasn't a personal relationship. I scored it a 3.5. They're not below me in rank, and we're a pretty formal organization, so I scored it a 1. I gave the good news question a 5. I truly think this is an exciting project. Total of 9.5. Pretty standard business. Made sense.

"I was clearly in the persuasive box of the Matrix of Persuasion—they could do what I asked if I could convince them to be on my side. Convincing them meant I needed to write about benefits.

"In terms of organizational structure, I realized that I had many options. I could have used the chronology organizational structure: first, I walked throughout the exhibit hall; second, I narrowed my field of potential vendors; third, I scheduled interviews, etc. I could have used the category organizational structure: exhibitors I met, educational programs I attended, etc.

PAR would have worked as well: my original assignment, the problem I was to address, the stated reason that they sent me to the conference, was to ID alternative vendors; I met with eight; attached is a summary of my recommendations. Even Q&A would have worked well: *Was attending the conference worthwhile?* Yes, it was an efficient way to interview potential vendors. *How many candidates did you consider?* Out of fourteen potential candidates, I met with eight."After considering all the organizational structures, I went with PAR. It has a powerful bottom-line orientation that suited my objective."

Notice how Elinor used the model in a step-by-step manner. "It was quick," she said. "Quick and easy. And because I used the model, I felt confident about the outcome."

2. You've been asked to inform senior managers about your department's progress in reaching a business objective. What organizational structure would you select?

Vic, a salesman in the chemical industry, said, "I absolutely hate writing, but I like presentations. So I figured that I'd create a simple one-page document summarizing my key points and distribute it during my presentation. Here's how I thought it through.

"My objective was to receive immediate feedback and praise about my presentation and our department's progress.

"Personality wise, our senior managers are all business. They're Producers. The progress we've made in our department is good, but management is impatient. So in terms of vocabulary, I wanted to talk about our big-picture plans and accomplishments. No details. I needed to have the details ready to go in case they asked for specifics, but my handout needed to satisfy their desire for a bottom-line orientation.

"My sense was that I could be relatively informal. Working with the Formality Index, I determined that I know them well and personally, so I scored the first question a 5. I am below them in rank, but I'm climbing the corporate ladder pretty quickly, so I gave the next question a 3. Realistically, I have really good news, so I gave the last question a 4.5. That totals to a 12.5, so I confirmed that an informal approach was fine.

"I thought this would be a pretty easy writing assignment. In terms of the Matrix of Persuasion, they were on my side and they could do what I was asking. Sure enough—easy. Knowing that was very reassuring.

"Regarding the organizational structure, I started with a statement of PAR, then used a category organizational structure. It was very logical, and by integrating some chronology as well, I was able to show how we were progressing in a systematic way toward the goal. It worked well."

3. You want to invite your team to your house for a social event. What organizational structure would you use?

Richard, a team leader in the banking industry, explained that once a year, he likes to invite his entire team to his house. "I started a new job and wanted to invite everyone over for a barbecue. My objective was to get people to RSVP and attend.

"The feature I wanted to focus on was that the team's families were welcome to the barbecue, that I understood that their jobs were only part of their lives. I manage three bank branches and have more than twenty people on the team. All personalities are represented, so I planned to use various phrases to speak to each.

"Regarding formality, given I'd just started my job, I didn't know them well. I scored the first question a 1.5. They were below me in rank, so I scored that question a 2. And it was absolutely good news, so I scored it a 5. That totaled 8.5. Lower than I'd expected. It implied quite a formal invitation, a little bit of a surprise to me considering it was a barbecue.

"I decided that this was a persuading challenge using the Matrix of Persuasion. Asking people to give up their own time for a semibusiness event, even a pleasurable one, well, I thought I'd need to be somewhat persuasive.

"I went through the organizational structures one by one, and I almost went with the category approach. It would have allowed me to focus on games the kids could play, food I would serve, and so on. Ultimately though, I decided to use chronology. I detailed the games and competitions by blocks of time. It looked fuller that way.

"I'd been thinking I would simply E-mail everyone, but then I decided to use some fun type fonts and produce a hard-copy invitation. I hand-delivered them as I traveled to each branch.

"People expressed pleasurable surprise that I took the time to produce a document."

ORGANIZE YOUR THINKING
USING AN OUTLINE OR HUB & SPOKES

Having selected an organizational structure, you're ready to put an outline or the Hub & Spokes model to work. The Hub & Spokes model is a visual, nonlinear way to organize your thinking and an alternative to traditional outlining.

No matter how complex the project, outlines and the Hub & Spokes model will help you get your most important ideas on paper—and you'll do it in about five to ten minutes.

Both systems, traditional outlining and the Hub & Spokes model, serve two purposes. They help you think things through and then create a logical sequence for your content.

Organize Your Thoughts
Methodically with a Traditional Outline

In a traditional outline, numerals and letters are used to create a hierarchy of information. Your primary points are labeled with large roman numerals. Subpoints under primary point use capital letters. The next level down uses regular numbers, followed by lowercase letters, and so on. Following the strict outlining conventions, you need at least two points within each category, although in business writing, there is far more flexibility.

Sarah, a director in a health care company, decided to send an E-mail to her team soliciting their ideas for a mandated budget reduction. "My objective was to receive E-mailed cost-cutting suggestions from all members of my team by my specified deadline.

"There's a wide variety of personalities, so I decided to use vocabulary to speak to all four personality types. I thought it made sense to highlight the benefit of being a team player to their individual careers. My Formality Index totaled ten, so I decided to be quite business-like in tone. I decided my challenge was problem solving according to the Matrix of Persuasion because no one was going to want to cut costs. I knew that I had to provide suggestions on how to approach the challenge in order to motivate the team to act, so I selected the PAR organizational structure.

"I like to outline. I'm very methodical by nature myself, so I work well with the tradition. Here's how it read:

I. Explain why they need to cut costs.
   A. Remind them that there's a corporate dictate that every department must cut costs.
      1. Refer to the CEO's memo.
      2. State the deadline.
   B. Add my endorsement that I believe we can maintain high quality while improving efficiency.
      1. Ask for ideas on how we can measure the effect of cost-cutting on quality.
      2. Ask for comments on how quality is measured now.
II. Ask for ideas on where they can cut costs.
   A. Tell them I'd look at travel and office supplies to start.
      1. Suggest that they look at trends in costs over the past three years.

2. Suggest that they correlate costs to revenue to see if cost increases resulted in increases in revenue.

B. Encourage them to be creative.

1. Announce that no categories are exempt from consideration.

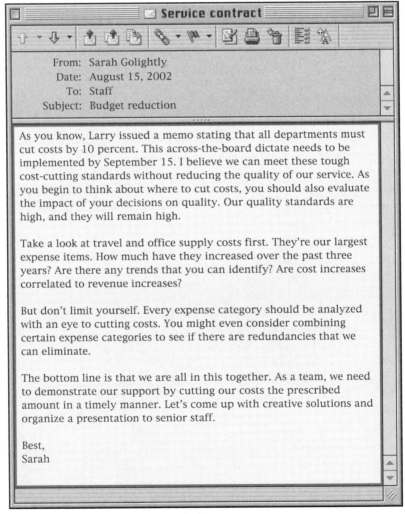

Figure 2.1 Budget Reduction E-mail

2. Suggest that they look at combining categories to see if we can eliminate duplications and redundancies.

"By identifying the main categories and forcing myself to fill in the blanks, I was able to generate ideas. For example, the idea of combining categories to avoid duplications and redundancies—I think that's a really good idea, and it only came to me because I needed a No. 2 to follow my No. 1. In the end, the E-mail just about wrote itself." (See Figure 2.1.)

Come Up with New Ideas Using the Hub & Spokes Model

Not everyone likes an outline. Charlie, a paralegal in a large law office, explains, "When I try to outline, I feel as if my brain is in a straight jacket. I go blank. It just doesn't work for me."

Hub & Spokes is an alternative approach. Instead of following a prescribed organizational format with strict hierarchical rules, Hub & Spokes allows you to follow your thoughts in an easy-to-track manner.

In the center of a blank piece of paper, draw a circle. Jot a summary of your objective and your audience in the circle. That's your hub: the essence of your communication challenge. Draw lines out from the circle. These spokes will serve as links from your hub to related thoughts.

Charlie, the paralegal, says, "I love the Hub & Spokes model. It works well for me. For example, I wanted to go to a seminar, but the firm had put a hold on all outside training. No surprise. Another example of cost reduction. The seminar was on document retention, so I knew it would be useful for our firm. But my boss said no, not now. Check back in six months. I didn't want to wait, so I decided to take one last crack at winning her approval.

"My objective was to have her say yes and authorize the expense. She's all Producer, very bottom-line oriented, so I needed to keep my eye on the ball. I knew a focus on the cost-savings benefit of learning what papers we didn't have to retain was key. In terms of formality, well, my score was nine, so a matter-of-fact memo seemed like a good idea. I thought about E-mail, but we're pretty conservative as a firm, and I didn't think that an E-mail would convey a serious enough image. Using the Matrix of Persuasion, clearly my challenge was to persuade.

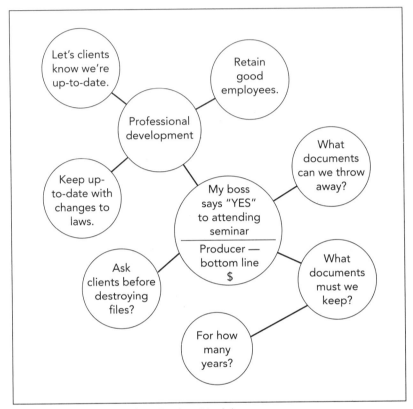

Figure 2.2 Charlie's Hub & Spokes Model

"I thought about using a category organizational structure, but went with PAR because it seemed easier. Here's my Hub & Spokes model (see Figure 2.2.)

"I was surprised that 'Professional Development' popped out of my head. If you'd asked me if I thought I should mention professional development in my efforts to persuade my boss, I'd have given you a flat-out no. But it came into my mind, so I wrote it down."

After completing the first level of spokes, Charlie picked "Professional Development" to work with next. "I was curious where it would lead me. When I focused on it, benefits to the firm came out of my head loud and clear. It's obvious that sending staff to seminars is one way to attract and keep good employees, but what is less obvious is that training employees is a selling point to clients. Clients need to know that the staff keeps up with changes in the laws.

"Suddenly, I realized I'd identified a benefit that was likely to be compelling to my Producer boss: attracting and retaining clients."

The Hub & Spokes model is a way of getting what's in your head on paper. The trick is not to edit yourself. As you work with it, you'll find that sometimes silly or unrelated comments occur to you. Write them down. You'll bring yourself back to the project at hand. Don't edit! Editing some comments may result in unintentionally editing others. So if "Oops! I forgot to take the chicken out of the freezer!" pops into your head, write "chicken" and "freezer" and move on. You'll bring yourself back on track.

Note that after writing your objective and a summary of your readers in the hub, your next step is to draw a few spokes. There's no specific number to draw or complete. When you run out of ideas, stop. Pick whichever spoke interests you, draw a circle around it, draw some spokes from it, and repeat the process. You keep going until you've jotted down all the relevant ideas that occur to you.

Charlie explains, "I didn't draw spokes out of any point except for 'Professional Development' because other points had already occurred to me, and I knew what I wanted to say about them."

Once you've completed the Hub & Spokes model to whatever level of detail you think is appropriate, decide which is your best point. That's usually where you want to start.

Notice that the first level of spokes represents your broad categories: paragraphs within a letter or report, for example, or sections within a proposal.

"Given my boss's orientation, I decided to start with the point about professional development. My memo began as follows:

> Given that clients demand that we be up-to-date with our knowledge of all relevant laws, attending a seminar to learn what documents must be retained on our clients' behalf is not an employee perk; it's critical to our firm's ability to maintain its leadership position.

"I went on to mention other benefits, for example, that we'd save money by not having to store unnecessary documents. And I ended with this:

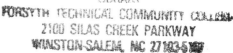

Bottom line: We need me to acquire this knowledge now.

"Guess what? My boss said yes. And she told me that my memo was really well written."

EXERCISE 6: *Get Your Thoughts Down on Paper*

You have been asked to write a reference letter for a colleague whom you respect and admire. Think about who this might be. It might be someone you went to school with, or it might be someone you have worked with in the past or work with now.

Whomever you choose, think about the job this person would logically be applying for at this point in his or her career. Think about the person who would be conducting the interview. That stranger—the person your colleague is hoping will hire him or her—is the person who has asked for this written reference.

1. What's your objective? For example, do you want the recipient of your reference letter to call you for further details?
2. What sort of personality would you expect the person you're writing to to have? You don't know the person, of course, but based on the job, what would you expect? (Remember that if you can't tell someone's personality, you target the Producer.)
3. Which of your colleague's attributes, skills, or abilities is likely to be of greatest value to a prospective employer?
4. How formal should the tone be?
5. In which quadrant of the Matrix of Persuasion does this project fall?
6. Which organizational structure should your letter employ?
7. Use either a traditional outline or the Hub & Spokes model to identify key points you want to make.

How did you do? Were you able to quickly go through the seven steps? Are you ready to write a first draft? In this chapter, we continued the process of getting our thoughts in order before we begin to write. We reviewed nine organizational structures, and we discussed two approaches to getting thoughts that are in your head down on paper. Now it's time to put pen to paper or fingers to keyboard.

CHAPTER THREE

Write Excellent First Drafts

WRITE POLISHED FIRST DRAFTS

In the last chapter, we compared nine organizational structures and considered which one to use under various circumstances, and whether to use each structure alone or in combination. We also discussed two systems for getting your thoughts in order: outlining and the Hub & Spokes model.

In this chapter, you'll learn three tools that will allow you to generate first drafts that are so polished, they mimic second drafts. The tools will help you save time by streamlining the initial revision process. Rather than create a rough first draft, it's more efficient to create a refined first draft. Your draft may still require revision, but the rewriting process will be easier and quicker because your draft has already integrated three standards of excellence:

1. a focus on your readers by maintaining a positive Empathy Index
2. a targeted salutation and high-impact lead to catch their interest
3. a response-generating close that motivates them to act

WRITE WITH YOUR READERS IN MIND

Given your writing is likely to be more effective if it is reader focused, you need to be able to assess whether your communication is focused too heavily on yourself or your organization. The Empathy Index measures reader focus. By comparing the number of references to your readers to the number of references to yourself or your organization, you get a snapshot of how benefit oriented your communication is and how engaging it is.

In order to calculate your Empathy Index, count the number of references to your target readers: "them." Count references to your readers by:

- pronouns
- shared interest
- use of their name or names
- inference

Next, count references to yourself and your organization: "us." (When the word "we" refers to both the reader and writer, don't count it.)

When the two numbers are subtracted ("us" from "them"), you should end up with a positive number. The higher the positive number, the more reader focused the writing. The more reader focused the writing, the more potent your communications are likely to be. Consider, for example, this sentence, drafted by a scientific laboratory:

We are pleased to announce that our new facility is open and ready to accept all microbiological tests.

Notice that there are no references to the lab's customers. But there are two references to the company ("we" and "our"). The Empathy Index is calculated as follows:

Them	0
Us	(2)
Empathy Index	−2

The same content presented in a much stronger way shifts the focus from the company to the company's customers. Consider this alternative:

Your microbiological tests will be turned around more quickly, and you'll enjoy a higher degree of accuracy than was previously available, because our new facility is now open and ready for your business.

In this example, there are three references to the company's customers ("your" twice and "you" once), but only one reference to the firm ("our").

Them	3
Us	(1)
Empathy Index	2

Try reading the two sentences aloud. The first sentence starts with a cliché that focuses on the company: "We are pleased to announce . . . " The revised sentence begins with benefits to the customer: "Your microbiological tests will be turned around more quickly . . . " Can you hear how much stronger the revised sentence is?

Refer to Your Readers Often

You'll recall that the four ways you can refer to your readers are by:

- pronouns
- shared interest
- use of their name or names
- inference

Whether you use one of these four techniques or all of them, it's crucial that you refer to your readers frequently—more often than you refer to yourself or your organization.

Aim to Use Dynamic Pronouns

Using the pronouns *you* and *your* is one of the easiest ways to focus on your readers. Consider the revised sentence discussed above:

Your microbiological tests will be turned around more quickly, and you'll enjoy a higher degree of accuracy than was previously available, because our new facility is now open and ready for your business.

Try starting a sentence using either *you* or *your* to announce that your new lab is open that *doesn't* mention a benefit. Go ahead, try it.

As soon as you turn the spotlight onto your readers, you invariably highlight issues that matter to them—benefits. Here are some examples of what other people have come up with by starting the sentence with the pronouns *you* or *your*:

- "Your business matters to us . . ."
- "Your concern for your patients is why we strive to achieve perfection . . ."
- "You know how important it is that your patients have trust in their test results . . ."

Note that each example focuses on an important issue of concern to readers—and expresses it as a benefit. The more benefits you write about, the more likely your readers are to read your material and ultimately respond as you ask.

Write About Shared Interests

Another approach to ensuring a positive Empathy Index to is to mention specific interests, activities, or experiences that your readers share. For example, instead of saying "The company is pleased to announce that the ABC software upgrade will be installed on Wednesday, allowing more research to be done in-house," say "Researchers will be glad to know that the ABC software upgrade will be installed on Wednesday, allowing more research to be done in-house." The term *researchers* is an example of a shared interest.

Think about what you and your readers have in common. Are you all members of the same team or group? Do you go fly-fishing with them? Are they interested in computer updates? Whatever the shared interest, activity, or experience, weave a reference or two about it into your writing to increase the impact of your message.

Use Your Readers' Names

Referring to your readers by name is one of the easiest ways to increase your Empathy Index. You need to be careful, however, because overuse of someone's name can sound like an affectation, as if you're a phony or obsequious.

In the discussion later in this chapter regarding salutations, you'll learn that using someone's name at the start of your communication is almost always a good idea (e.g., Dear George, or Dear Dr. Janson). You might also consider closing with a reference to your reader or readers (e.g., "Thanks again, Matthew, for your assistance.").

Be cautious, however, about using references in the body of a letter or other communication. Adding references risks conveying an overly familiar, even servile attitude.

Don't be discouraged from referring to people by name; just be certain the tone is appropriate. One way to do this is to read the text aloud, pretending that you are having a conversation with your reader. If it sounds natural in conversation, probably it's appropriate in writing.

Using a category that refers to your readers, such as a job title, can be a viable alternative to naming someone. This approach is effective when it's impractical to write to individuals because there are too many of them. For example, in a newsletter article or a press release, the text needs to reach a broad audience. Saying "Employees with more than five years' service need to update their forms" is an example of referring to a specific segment of the population, in this case, all employees with more than five years' service.

Capitalize on the Power of Inference

Starting sentences with a verb, a writing technique using the imperative mood, is a forceful way to make a point, and it implies the pronoun *you*. For example, if you write, "Attend the meeting and let me know whether an agreement is reached," the reference to your reader is understood. You're really saying, "*You* attend the meeting and *you* let me know whether an agreement is reached." In this example, note that we would count two references to your reader, because you are implying the pronoun *you* twice.

The imperative is a tried-and-true approach that reaches your readers in a strong and directive manner. By using a forceful tone, you imply an urgency that encourages a response.

In some circumstances, the imperative is not appropriate. For instance, in an E-mail to your boss, you might not be comfortable saying "Review the attached report." Because the imperative sounds like you're issuing an order, most people wouldn't be comfortable addressing their boss in this manner. Instead, soften the imperative by writing "Please review the attached report." That one word, "Please," adjusts your tone sufficiently and still maintains a strong appeal. Use your judgment about when to add the word *please*.

One approach to making the decision is to read the text aloud; if it sounds too brusque, add the word *please*. Contrast these examples:

Call today.	Please call today.
Fill out the form.	Please fill out the form.
Attend the meeting.	Please attend the meeting.

Notice how adding *please* allows you to achieve a friendly, polite tone without diminishing the strong, directive attitude that comes from using the imperative.

You might phrase the announcement of the new microbiology lab as "Send us your microbiology tests and discover the difference in quality and speed our new facility makes." Or you could say, "Please send us your microbiology tests and discover the difference in quality and speed our new facility makes." Which do you prefer? Some people feel that the tone is less professional when you add the word *please* in this circumstance, almost as if you're begging. Others think it's courteous and more formal. Neither is right, just as neither is wrong in this example; the sentences have a different feel from one another, that's all.

Part of your decision will be based on your comfort level. Not everyone is comfortable using the authoritative tone of the imperative. And some people perceive that using *please* adds a tone of pleading that sounds unprofessional in standard business writing. Use your best judgment on a case-by-case basis.

Sometimes you imply a reference to the reader by constructing your sentence to create a sense of connection between you, the writer, and your readers. For example, in the sentence "It's important to check your credit on an annual basis," you're implying a reference to the reader. Depending on the target audience, this sentence is really saying "It's important (if you own a home) to check your credit on an annual basis," or "It's important (if you intend to buy a home) to check your credit on an annual basis," or "It's important (for you) to check your credit on an annual basis."

Implying a reference to your readers is a subtle and effective technique, and it serves to increase your Empathy Index.

Vary the Pace While Increasing Your Empathy Index

A positive Empathy Index ensures that your writing is benefit oriented and reader focused. You can use any of the four techniques, or you can use a combination of the four. For example, notice how all four approaches are integrated in the following memo from Mary Jo, a crises hot line executive director, to the hot line's volunteers. Mary Jo uses pronouns, refers to shared interest, addresses her readers by job title, and allows inference to her readers to be made as well.

Dear Volunteers:

It's easy to skip paperwork. Caring people like you, people who volunteer for work on a hot line, are there to do the work—to provide the kindness callers need. When we ask you to use forms and fill out reports, we know it's hard for you to muster enthusiasm.

Good news! Volunteers report that the new log sheets are easy to complete. Sure, there are growing pains, and we need to work out a few bugs, but all in all the forms are doing what we need them to do: track calls and provide broad statistical data.

You have been terrific in your openness to change and in your support in helping us achieve this quality objective that has been essential to the program's success. Any questions? Please call me directly. And again, thank you, thank you.

Warmly, Mary Jo

Doesn't the memo read well? It's clear, upbeat, and reader focused.

EXERCISE 7: *Calculate the Empathy Index*
Calculate the Empathy Index for the memo on page 57. Then count the number of references to the executive director's readers (by name,

shared interest, inference, or pronoun). Then count the number of references to the director or the hot line itself. When you subtract the number of references to Mary Jo or the hot line from the number of references to the reader, are you left with a positive number?

After you have completed your analysis, compare your assessment and Empathy Index to Mary Jo's. Then take a look at Mary Jo's explanation of how she approached writing the memo. (The references to the reader are in boldface and the references to Mary Jo and the hot line are underlined.)

Dear **Volunteers:**

It's easy (**implied "for you"**) to skip paperwork. **Caring people like you, people who volunteer for work on a hot line**, are there to do the work—to provide the kindness (**implied "you are there to provide the kindness"**) callers need. When <u>we</u> ask **you** to use forms and fill out reports, <u>we</u> know it's hard for **you** to muster enthusiasm.

Good news! **Volunteers** report that the new log sheets are easy to complete. Sure, there are growing pains, and <u>we</u> need to work out a few bugs, but the forms are doing what <u>we</u> need them to do: track calls and provide broad statistical data.

You have been terrific in **your** openness to change and in **your** support in helping <u>us</u> achieve this quality objective that has been essential to the program's success. Any questions? Please call <u>me</u> (**implied "You call me"**) directly. And again, thank **you**, thank **you**.

Warmly, <u>Mary Jo</u>

Them	14
Us	(7)
Empathy Index	7

Seven is a strong score, and you can hear it in the upbeat tone of the memo. Note the variety of approaches Mary Jo used: the pronoun "you," the reference to the job category (i.e., "volunteers"), the reference to shared interest (i.e., "caring people"), and the imperative (i.e., "Please call me").

Using this variety of reader references adds liveliness and reader interest to the memo. Mary Jo signaled a strong connection with her volunteers by referring to them in so many different ways.

Mary Jo said, "I was very conscious of the Empathy Index as I created the first draft. Being aware of it saved me a lot of time. I found that I'd pause between sentences and consider how I could integrate one or more of the four options for referring to my readers. At the time, I thought these pauses would add up to extra time in writing. But no—it actually saved me time.

"When I write, typically I know *what* I want to say. What was new to me in the writing process was to pause and think for a moment about *how* I wanted to say it. The idea of adding a reference to my readers in every sentence, if I could, was new to me. Soon it became second nature, and I discovered that my first drafts were so much better than they used to be that it took me less time to revise them—which means the memo writing process became quicker once I got used to the system. By writing better, more focused first drafts, I've reduced the time it takes me to write a decent communication by about a third."

EXERCISE 8: *Rewrite to Improve the Empathy Index*

In the E-mail below from Paula, a manager, to Jim, an engineer, calculate the Empathy Index. Then, using the techniques discussed above, rewrite it to increase the Empathy Index.

Hi **Jim**:

I am writing in response to yesterday's conference call in which I was embarrassed that I wasn't up-to-date in my information about the ABC Corporation deal. I think it's important that we address this issue right away.

First, ABC said that I need to coordinate with you more effectively to save them the job of repeating conversations. This was pretty humiliating to me as you and I certainly ought to be in close touch about this customer.

Second, I expect you to keep me up-to-date at every step along the way. I expect you to do that without my having to hear updates from the customer.

Best, Paula

How did you evaluate the Empathy Index? The following is one assessment. (Note that the references to Jim are in boldface and the references to Paula are underlined.)

Hi **Jim**:

I am writing in response to yesterday's conference call in which I was embarrassed that I wasn't up-to-date in my information about the ABC Corporation deal. I think it's important that we address this issue right away.

First, ABC said that I need to coordinate with **you** more effectively to save them the job of repeating conversations. This was pretty humiliating to me as **you** and I certainly ought to be in close touch about this customer.

Second, I expect **you** to keep me up-to-date at every step along the way. I expect **you** to do that without my having to hear updates from the customer.

Best, Paula

Note that there were five references to Jim (the reader) and thirteen references to Paula (the writer), resulting in a negative Empathy Index (five minus thirteen equals negative eight).

Them	5
Us	(13)
Empathy Index	−8

Consider the writer's objective. What does Paula want Jim to do? Remember to express her objective as an action step.

What did you decide is Paula's objective? Isn't it true that Paula wants Jim to cooperate, contact her with news, and include her in meetings and updates?

With that objective in mind, rewrite the E-mail to ensure a positive Empathy Index.

It's easy to be distracted from our objective by our emotions. Listen to Paula's perspective. "The situation *was* embarrassing and humiliating. I had no idea whether Jim was keeping me in the dark because he was trying to sabotage me or he was incompetent, but I knew I had to do something. My instinct was to attack—read my first draft.

"The Empathy Index saved me from making the situation worse by forcing me to keep my focus on what was important. Rather than berate Jim, a pointless exercise, it made more sense for me to maintain a calm tone."

As you'll see in the upcoming chapters, there are lots of approaches to revising first drafts. We've seen that there are several ways to write well. You'll see that there are several ways to revise well, too. Here is Paula's revision:

Hi **Jim**:

Thank **you** for including <u>me</u> on yesterday's conference call. After the call, it's clear that **you** and <u>I</u> need to come up with a system that ensures <u>I'm</u> kept up-to-date on ABC business—we need to coordinate more effectively. How do **you** think **you'd** like to handle this? Would **you** keep <u>me</u> up-to-date at every step along the way? Let's meet tomorrow to discuss a plan
of action.

Best, <u>Paula</u>

Note that adding references to Jim forced Paula to write less emotionally—always a good idea in business With the new focus on Jim and his needs, the Empathy Index became positive. (Note that the references to Jim ["them"] are in boldface and the references to Paula ["us"] are underlined. The word "we" isn't counted because it refers to both Jim and Paula. Likewise, the word "Let's" [i.e., "Let us"] isn't counted for the same reason.)

Them	6
Us	<u>(5)</u>
Empathy Index	1

Not only does the E-mail become more positive, it also becomes more action oriented, and as such, is much more likely to achieve Paula's objective: for Jim to include her in updates.

YOUR SALUTATION AND LEAD SET THE TONE

How you refer to your readers signals the level of formality you intend to convey. People read salutations for the clues they provide about what's to follow in both tone and content. Readers depend on the lead to engage their interest.

If either the salutation or the lead is off-key or inappropriate, you're likely to lose your readers' interest. On the other hand, if the salutation and the lead are on the mark, you're likely to engage your readers' interest and attention.

Use the Salutation to Connect with Your Readers

The best salutation is the reader's name. Unquestionably, referring directly to people by name is the strongest possible beginning.

The following are the strongest to weakest salutations:

1. individual name
2. specific shared interest
3. broad category
4. generic formula

A Person's Name Is Dear to Them

You have many options in salutations, from using someone's name to employing the generic "To Whom It May Concern." When you start a letter or other communication with someone's name, you signal to that person that you know who he or she is. That connection encourages the person to read on.

In certain circumstances, you should adhere to formal protocol. Specifically, when writing letters to any member of the diplomatic corps, the military, or elected officials, it's usually best to adhere strictly to the standards of protocol. (Consult the "Forms of Address" section in many standard dictionaries and business etiquette books.)

In most business applications, however, there's a range of acceptable salutations. It's important that you think carefully about this issue because the decisions you make will set the overall tone of your communication and can encourage readership.

Spell Names Correctly

It goes without saying that if you use people's names, you need to be certain that you've spelled them correctly. A misspelled name implies a lack of care or concern, sloppiness, or incompetence. Be careful to get it right.

The only way to confirm the proper spelling of a name is to call and ask. Simply copying a name from a directory or a phone book, for example, only proves that you have transcribed the name accurately, not that you have written the correct name. Also, people's names change. In other words, even if the directory spelling is correct and you transcribe the name properly, you may still get the name wrong—perhaps a woman has married or gotten divorced, for instance.

Savi, a clerk in a human resources department says, "I recently met a woman whose last name was Enfield. She came into the office to change her health insurance to an individual policy. She had just gotten divorced and gone back to her maiden name. You never know. A month ago her name was Terry Wren, now it's Terry Enfield."

Some companies have found that response increases so much when they address people by name that it's worth their while to have staff call and verify every name, even for large mailings. Whatever you decide to do, whenever you use someone's name, it's critical that you get it right.

Be Appropriately Formal

One issue that you need to consider is whether to use first or last names. In our informal society, it is common to use first names even when we don't know people well. A better choice, however, is to use last names until you have established a relationship.

Many people are offended by the presumption of intimacy that results from an inappropriate use of someone's first name. A letter from a stranger addressing you by your first name may not receive the kind of attention the sender seeks. "I throw those letters away," Tom says. "As general manager of a lens manufacturing company, I get dozens of pitch letters a week. My assistant weeds out most of the junk, but sometimes a couple reach my desk. I look at them. If they start 'Dear Tom' and I don't even know the company or the writer, forget it. Straight into the trash. They make me mad. Maybe I'm old fashioned, but that's how I feel."

Sally, a business student approaching graduation and now on a job hunt, explains that she applies for most positions online. "I hesitate to say 'Dear Mr. Smith' in an E-mail, but I do it. I don't know Mr. Smith, so I figure it's best to be more formal, rather than less formal."

Sally's right. Even in an E-mail, usually if you don't know the person you're writing to personally, you shouldn't use his or her first name. There are exceptions, of course. A new supervisor, for example, might send an E-mail saying hello to each of her employees and use each person's first name, even before she's met them individually, to set a tone of approachability.

As a general rule, though, it's better to err on the side of extra formality, rather than insufficient formality.

Speak to an Interest You Share

Sometimes it's not cost-effective to use people's names. In some mass mailings, for example, even with a mail-merge capability, the cost of adding individual names may not be deemed an appropriate expenditure. Instead, ask yourself why you're writing to these people and how that relates to something they want or need. By honing in on why your readers might want to read your communication, it becomes easier to identify what the shared interest is.

Julia, a manager of software development at a midsize computer company, explained, "I was writing an E-mail to my group. I could have said 'Dear Team' or 'Dear Development Group.' Instead I focused on the subject matter of the E-mail, which was a query about whether we were going to be able to meet a critical deadline. Given the hours we had put in, and especially the analysts who had been working fifty- and sixty-hour weeks to complete this phase of the project, I used 'Dear Anyone Interested in Working Fewer Hours.' Not only did it help the E-mail get read, but it got a laugh. Always a good thing when you're stressed about meeting a deadline."

Notice that Julia highlighted an area of shared interest to the readers: working fewer hours.

Use Specifics Within General Categories

If you're unable to find a narrow shared interest that applies to all readers, you'll need to select a broad category. Categories that are generic should be avoided. "Dear Friend," "Dear Donor," or "Dear Citizen," for example, are usually ineffective salutations. They're too broad to speak to an individual.

Hong-Thing, president of a parent-teacher organization said, "I wanted to send a letter home with all of the children asking their parents to attend a potluck supper where we'll be able to discuss the city council's proposed cutbacks in an informal atmosphere. I considered addressing the letters to 'Dear Parent' but thought I could do better. Instead of 'Dear Parent,' I selected 'Dear Concerned Parent.' My thinking was that it would speak more forcefully to those parents who were concerned—that is, most parents."

"Dear Concerned Parent" is not ideal. It would be better to address each parent by name. But that's not realistic. Hong-Thing is a volunteer, and taking the time to address each letter individually isn't possible. Nor does she think it's necessary. "My letter is informational. I can't imagine that a parent would be more likely to read the invitation or respond because it began with an individual name."

If You Use a Generic Salutation, Stay with the Standards

Least effective of all is a generic salutation. However, there are times when it's the best solution. In standard business letters making a common request, for example, a generic salutation may be the most appropriate way to go.

Frank needed to request a replacement hose for his vacuum cleaner. "The vacuum cleaner company had announced that the hose was defective and customers could send for a free replacement. Starting the letter with 'To Whom It May Concern' was easy and effective."

The salutation "To Whom It May Concern" has been the standard for generations and is still appropriate. You can also use "Dear Sir or Madam." What you should avoid are old-fashioned salutations that are likely to alienate some of your readers. "Gentlemen," for example, or "Dear Sir" should be avoided, for obvious reasons.

HOOK YOUR READERS' INTEREST WITH A COMPELLING LEAD

The first several words or phrases of your communication are called the lead or lead-in. If the lead doesn't catch your readers' attention, it's unlikely they'll read on. Why would they? To have your objectives met, you need to have your material read.

Follow the Rule of First Reference

No matter how high you score on the Empathy Index, no matter how strong your reader focus, try to adhere to the Rule of First Reference, which says that your first reference should be to your readers, not yourself.

It's not always possible to do, but if you can, it's a good idea. Compare these two leads:

I am pleased to report that last year's numbers are better than expected.

versus

Thanks to your hard work, last year's numbers are better than expected.

Note that the first example isn't terrible or incorrect; rather, it's better writing to focus on your readers before you mention yourself or your organization. Sometimes avoiding the pronouns "I," "my," "our," and any other direct reference to you or your company forces you to be more concise and to the point.

For example, in reference letters, it's common to begin with a reference to yourself. Look what happens, though, when you avoid doing so.

Instead of "It is my great pleasure to recommend Gregory Jones as a member of your strategic team. His financial acumen will help the team calculate ROI and break-even, and his upbeat personality will help keep a smile on everyone's faces," say "Your strategic team will benefit in tangible and intangible ways if Gregory Jones joins the group. His financial acumen will help the team calculate ROI and break-even, and his upbeat personality will help keep a smile on everyone's faces. It is my great pleasure to recommend him."

The difference is subtle. It's not that the first lead is bad or wrong; rather, it is better to start with benefits.

There are three approaches to writing a lead that work well in business communications:

1. Start with a time-sensitive word or phrase.
2. Allude to a shared interest.
3. Pose a question.

No matter which lead style you use, it's important that you think about the beginning of your communications.

Use Time-Sensitive Vocabulary to Increase Urgency

Certain time-related words and phrases inspire action, such as "now," "today," "before the deadline passes," "right away," "time is of the essence," and "by the end of business today" (or "in an hour," or by any other specified deadline). This time-sensitive vocabulary creates a sense of urgency while maintaining a professional, business-like tone.

While the above and similar phrases create a sense of timeliness, try to avoid the clichéd generic phrase "as soon as possible" (or its abbreviation, ASAP). It is ineffective. Instead, integrate the effective words and phrases listed above into the content of your communications. Consider the following examples:

"Three o'clock is the deadline for submissions . . ."

"Your report raised several important issues that I want to review with you within the next several days."

"Before we meet tomorrow, we need to . . ."

"By the end of the day, I'll need a full accounting of . . ."

"Now that I've reviewed your proposal, I have several questions . . ."

"Call Ms. Carter right away and assure her of our full support."

Can you hear the sense of urgency that's implied? In each example, the terminology is natural. The sentence flows. It sounds right. That's good writing.

EXERCISE 9: *Add Urgency Through Time-Sensitive Vocabulary*
Rewrite the E-mail lead (the first phrase or sentence) below to integrate a time-sensitive word or phrase.

Hi Team:

According to Max and Jonathan, the ABC Company has accepted our proposal pending clarification of a few issues. This is great news, and we want to be sure to address their concerns pronto! Let's go over the specifics at 9 a.m. tomorrow. Confirm with Cathy that you'll be there.

Jan

What do you think? Did you notice the salutation? Starting an E-mail with "Hi" instead of the more traditional "Dear" signals a less formal tone. Using the category salutation "team" is a good way of indicating a group purpose.

Go ahead. Calculate the Empathy Index, then compare your assessment with the following analysis. (References to the team are in boldface and the reference to Jan, the writer, is underlined. Note that references to "we," and "our" aren't counted because they include both the team and Jan.)

Hi **Team**:

Great news—but an urgent client request awaits our attention. According to Max and Jonathan, the ABC Company has accepted our proposal pending clarification of a few issues. Let's go over the specifics at 9 a.m. tomorrow. We want to be sure to address their concerns pronto! **Confirm** with Cathy that **you'll** be there.

<u>Jan</u>

Them	3
Us	(1)
Empathy Index	1

What about the time-sensitive vocabulary? Did you notice some of Jan's excellent word choices? How about "pronto"? It's an unusual, attention-getting word. But it's not specific. It's a fancy way of saying "as soon as possible." It's vague. Specifying the meeting's starting time is good, but how about adding a deadline for letting Cathy know if they'll be attending?

With these ideas in mind, what do you think of Jan's final version?

> Hi **Team**:
>
> Great news! We've just learned that the ABC Company has accepted our proposal. According to Max and Jonathan the company requires clarification of a few issues. We want to be sure to address their concerns pronto! I expect us to E-mail them the answers by the end of business tomorrow. Let's go over the specifics at 9 a.m. tomorrow. **Confirm** with Cathy by 5 p.m. today that **you'll** be there.
>
> Jan

Jan added several time-sensitive words and phrases, including specifying when the customer response is due and when the team members need to let Cathy know if they'll be attending the morning meeting. The Empathy Index is lower but still positive:

Them	3
Us	(2)
Empathy Index	1

As with all writing, there are multiple options here. Jan's original E-mail was good; most people agree that her revision is better, and final version better still. Remember, don't ever feel as if you're on a hunt for the one "right" way of saying something.

ADD A SNAPPY CLOSE

A close refers to the last sentence or two of your document as well as how you sign off. Closings should do two things: Summarize the action you want your readers to take and signal your level of formality. Also, in closing you need to consider whether you want to include a P.S., attachments, or an addendum.

Motivate Your Readers to Action

Some professional writers say that they write their last sentence first—so they'll always know where they're heading. It's an interesting approach. Think about it this way: You expressed your purpose in writing as a statement of action—your objective. By writing the end first, you can use it to guide you as you write your communication.

For example, if your objective is *to have all team members submit their activity reports by the 15th of the month,* you might consider closing your message by saying "Your activity reports are due no later than March 15."

Notice what we didn't say: If you have any questions, please feel free to call. This is a cliché and ineffective. If, in fact, you want to end with a statement like that, make it specific: "If you have any questions, I'm available at (phone number here) between 2:00 and 4:00 most afternoons." Specificity adds interest and encourages action.

The following three approaches to closing your communications are proven techniques:

1. Give a specific action instruction.
2. End with a question.
3. Close where it ends naturally.

Select the style of closing that's appropriate for the media, your objective, and your personal style.

Tell Your Readers What to Do Next
Giving a specific action instruction increases the likelihood that your readers will act.

For example, Maureen, benefits manager in the human resources department of a paper manufacturer, wrote an article for her company's employee newsletter about mutual fund options newly available in the 401(k) retirement plan. "We were scared that the floodgates would open and we'd be overwhelmed with calls," she explained. "So I ended the article by saying: 'For further information about the new options, to review your account, or to E-mail questions to a benefits manager, please click on the 401(k) icon on our intranet's home page.'"

Tim, a lawyer in an energy distributorship, wanted his staff to review legal findings before their upcoming meeting. "I sent an E-mail telling them that I wanted them to read several cases before we met. I gave them two that I expected them to read, and ended with 'Consult Marianna for additional case suggestions.' I was interested in tracking who consulted Marianna and who didn't."

"In a proposal we sent out," Malcolm, vice president of a construction company, explains, "for our engineering design services, we ended each section with source information. For instance, in the financial section, the last sentence was 'All data provided by the U.S. Department of the Interior. Please consult their website for details.' Very matter-of-fact, which was exactly the tone we wanted."

Ginny, owner of a restaurant supply company, sent out letters to all her customers announcing a price increase. "I explained it in the body of the letter, and ended with 'Attached is an updated price listing for your binder. Please replace the current page with this one.' Short and sweet."

Challenge Your Readers with a Question
Ending with a question involves readers by inviting them to think.

"I wanted to challenge people to come up with ideas," Max says. Creative director of an internal advertising department in the textile industry, Max ended a staff E-mail looking for new promotional ideas with "T-shirts and baseball caps. Tote bags and pens. We need a fresh approach. Any ideas?" He explained, "Ending with a question helps people focus."

Sarah, a freelance writer, wanted to win approval for an article idea. She ended her E-mailed inquiry to an editor with "Any interest?" As she explains, "That's the bottom line. It's to the point, and that's what editors like."

Finish Naturally

Allowing your text to end where it ends naturally is an easy and effective technique.

"I ran out of things to say," explains Fred, a graphic designer. "I was writing a proposal to get a new computer setup. I'd made my points clearly and needed to end with a bang. Using the list of closing approaches as a checklist was very helpful. The action I wanted my boss to take was obvious and saying something like 'Call me and authorize this purchase' is totally inappropriate. I considered closing with a question. I thought about ending with 'May I proceed?' But even that seemed too aggressive. My boss wouldn't like it. So finally, I just let it end where I ran out of things to say. The last line was 'With this setup, we'll have the most advanced capabilities the industry has to offer.'"

Karla, a physical therapist, says that she always used to end her letters with "If you have any questions, please feel free to contact me." She says, "Not only is it trite, but honestly, I didn't want to invite questions because clients take me up on it, and I never get off the phone. No action was necessary, no question seemed appropriate. So I just let the letters end where they naturally end. It seems to work well."

Whatever technique you choose, pay attention to the close. Many people scan—don't read—communications. They'll look at the salutation, the lead, and then go directly to the close. It's an important component and you need to take advantage of its potential.

Signal Formality with Your Sign-Off

Traditional forms of ending a communication include *Sincerely* and *Yours truly*. Modern but still professional forms include *Regards*, *With regards*, *Best regards*, and *Cordially*.

Using the traditional forms of ending your communication creates a formal tone. Employing more modern forms generates an informal tone. Consult your Formality Index from Chapter One to decide which approach is best.

With the traditional forms, you generally sign (or type in an E-mail) your full name. With modern forms, you may sign your full name or only your first name.

Add More Information

Consider whether to use a P.S. in your letters and whether to add attachments to a proposal or report.

A P.S. provides one last opportunity to make your primary message clear. Attachments flesh out documents and allow readers to find specific information that may be of great interest to them but which may be of limited interest to most people.

A P.S. Gets Read

A P.S. is most effective when it reiterates what action you want your readers to take, and what they'll get if they do what you ask.

For example, Amanda, an accounts receivable manager in a bank, used a P.S. in her collection letters. "I'd often say something like, 'Thanks for seeing that account #1234 is brought up-to-date, or call me directly at ext. 321 to avoid further action being taken.' It's not overly aggressive, but the implication is clear. Pay me or call me, or else."

One advantage of using a P.S. is that there's a good chance it will be read. People who scan letters are more likely to read your P.S. than the body of your letter. If you decide to add a P.S., summarize your best benefit and remind readers of the action to take.

Attachments Signal Substance

Attachments add length. Adding length helps the document seem more complete or significant. Even if no one refers to the attachments or reads them, it might make sense to include them because of the perception of substance they convey.

Components to add to a proposal or report might include:

- a copy of your organization's warranty or guarantee
- your company's mission statement
- the executive team or principals' résumés or CVs
- the data or statistics on which your recommendations are based
- several testimonials, references, or endorsements
- a resource list
- bibliography and endnotes

If you add attachments to supplement the body of your work, be certain to include a table of contents so readers can find those sections of interest to them and skip the rest. Even if all the attachments are skipped, simply including them adds weight—literally and figuratively—to your communications.

Attaching documents to E-mails, on the other hand, needs to be carefully considered. Many companies have security programs that flag E-mails with attachments. Worries about viruses and policies prohibiting the circulation of jokes and cartoons have resulted in many organizations stopping E-mails with attachments from reaching the intended party without first going to a security administrator. Make sure your readers know the attachment is relevant and expected.

EXERCISE 10: *Write a First Draft*

You're now ready to write a first draft. In Chapter Two, you created an outline or a Hub & Spokes model for a reference letter for a colleague. Review your outline or model to remind yourself of the points you want to make. What is your most compelling benefit? Where do you want to start? What's your objective?

While there are countless ways to write a letter of reference, effective ones share some qualities: a sincere tone, relevant information, and an offer to follow up.

Get your thoughts in order, answer the questions below, and get ready to write! Don't worry if you go blank. Simply draw a circle around the word or phrase you're struggling with (or on a computer, type xx). In the revision process we'll come back and figure out what to do with your circles (and we'll search for your xx's).

Don't worry about grammar, spelling, or sentence length—that is, don't worry about the details. Focus on your subject matter, and then write.

1. How will you refer to your reader? By first name? By last name? What salutation is appropriate?
2. Write a lead. How do you want to begin your letter? Can you incorporate the Rule of First Reference?
3. How do you want to end? What's your conclusion?
4. Will you end with Sincerely? Regards? Do you intend to sign your full name?

5. Do you want to add a P.S.? Do you want to attach any additional material? If so, what and why?
6. Ready? Write a draft of the letter.

How did it feel to write the draft? Most people find that thinking first, then writing, equips them to write better communications in less time.

In this chapter, we covered how to maintain a reader focus with the Empathy Index. We discussed how to begin and end your communications, and whether you should add a P.S. or an attachment. Now we're ready to begin to correct and improve your work. In the next chapter, you'll learn about tools that will speed the revision process.

CHAPTER FOUR

Hands-on Writing Workshop

ADD CREDIBILITY AS YOU REVISE

In the last chapter, you learned to use tools to write polished first drafts. You were able to use the Empathy Index to ensure that your communications have a strong reader focus. You selected targeted salutations and leads to help engage your readers' interest, and you compared alternative closings and worked to increase urgency by using time-sensitive words and phrases.

In this chapter, we're going to use two tools to begin the revision process. The two tools are:

1. adding specificity with numbers, facts, and examples
2. using the FURY principle to select words and phrases that best express your meaning

You'll learn that you aren't on a hunt for the one and only good way to revise your communications; on the contrary, you'll discover that there are many effective approaches to expressing your thoughts.

SPECIFICS INCREASE BELIEVABILITY

In Chapter One, we discussed the Matrix of Persuasion and made the point that most business communications are persuasive in nature. Your communications need to be convincing. Whatever your objective, in order to encourage action, you need to persuade your readers that what you say is true.

Even messages that are more informational and matter-of-fact than persuasive need to be believable. Your sincerity and passion need to come through in order to motivate your readers to act. One of the ways you can achieve a professional tone is by adding specific details. Numbers, facts, statistics, examples, and illustrations all contribute to the credibility of your communications. Weave them into your text to increase believability and the impact of your communications.

Add Numbers or Statistics in Every Sentence

Generalities are hard to understand, and often they're dull and uninteresting. Converting general statements into specific statements engages readers' interest by increasing believability. One of the easiest ways to add specificity is to add numbers or statistics.

For example, if you send an E-mail to your boss informing him or her that the holiday party you were charged with organizing will come in under budget, that's good news, but some bosses might say that it sounds too good to be true. If, however, you report that the holiday party will come in $467.32 under budget, that's credible. Adding the specific number automatically enhances believability.

Instead of "Everyone had a good time at the conference," say "Ninety-four percent of conference participants reported they had an excellent or very good time." Instead of "The need for creative waste management solutions is increasing each year," say "With solid waste increasing at over 14 percent a year, the need for creative waste management solutions becomes more urgent each year."

Henry, who owns a commercial printing company, explains that he writes collection letters to customers whose bills are overdue. "When an account is more than forty-five days past due, I send a letter. I used to say, 'Your account is overdue.' Now I say, 'Your account is more than fifty-two days overdue.' Adding the number of days makes my letter more powerful."

Notice that small changes generate big benefits. As you read the following alternative sentences, consider which one of each pair is more credible.

1. The summer picnic was well attended.
2. Sixty-seven employees attended the summer picnic.

1   After completing the attached forms, submit them for credit approval.
2. After completing the attached five forms, submit them for credit approval.

1. Mandy Jones had questions about the proposal.
2. Mandy Jones had three questions about the proposal.

Adding numbers is an easy way to beef up your content. It helps people understand your points and makes the text more believable.

EXERCISE 11: *Add Specificity to General Statements*

In the following example, rewrite the text by adding numbers or statistics. Read the explanatory paragraph, and then revise to add specificity.

Harriet, president of a floral supply company, wants to send an E-mail to motivate her employees to do their best work despite gloomy economic conditions. Six months ago, all associates in her company had their pay cut by 5 percent; managers had their pay cut by 15 percent. Although business is still down, Harriet wants to report a slight upswing in advance orders, which she hopes is the first glimmer of a full recovery. Three new customers have placed orders in the past month. If the trend continues, she anticipates that the company will be able to reinstate pay soon—perhaps as soon as the next quarter.

She is concerned, however, because customer complaints have risen. More than twenty complaints came in during the last quarter. That's nearly double the previous quarter and 40 percent higher than a year ago. Harriet is concerned that employees are slacking off. She wants them to know the future of the company, and thus their jobs, is directly tied to providing excellent customer service and if they slack off, customers will go elsewhere.

Here's Harriet's first draft:

Hi Team:

As you know, this has been the most difficult period in the company's history. We all had to share the pain—every one of us has had our pay cut. Things are beginning to look a little brighter, but we all need to be certain that the turnaround is solid and work to our highest capacity.

I have become concerned that an increase in customer complaints reflects a slacking off on the part of some employees. If you slack off, our recovery will be hindered. It's crucial that you do your best every day on every job.

I'll keep you posted about the recovery. With any luck, we'll be able to reverse the pay cuts soon. If there are any issues that you'd like to discuss with me, I encourage you to do so. E-mail or call me directly.

Harriet

What did you think of Harriet's E-mail? Most people think it's pretty good. It's benefit oriented and reader focused (scoring a seven on the Empathy Index). It has a good lead and the close suggests specific action. It adheres to the standards of excellence we've discussed thus far. What it lacks, however, is specifics. Review the paragraphs above the E-mail to remind yourself of the facts and numbers that are available, and revise Harriet's E-mail to add specificity.

How did you do? Were you able to integrate several numbers into the text? As you read your revision, can you hear how every sentence sounds stronger and more believable when numbers and statistics are included?

There are several effective ways to revise Harriet's E-mail. Here's one:

Hi Team:

As you know, this has been the most difficult period in the company's history. We've all had to share the pain—every one of us has had our pay cut, some by as much as 15 percent. With three new customers in the past month placing orders, things are beginning to look a little brighter, but we all need to be certain that the turnaround is solid and work to our highest capacity.

I have become concerned about an increase in customer complaints—more than twenty complaints were received in the last quarter, more than double the number of complaints we received the quarter before. While I know that morale is low, some employees aren't taking the same care that they used to. If you don't do your best, our recovery will be hindered. It's crucial that you do your best every day on every job.

I'll keep you posted about the recovery. With any luck, we'll be able to reinstate full pay soon, perhaps as soon as the next quarter. If there are any issues that you'd like to discuss with me, I encourage you to do so. E-mail or call me directly.

Harriet

Simply adding a few numbers makes the entire message clearer and more compelling.

Ground General Information with Examples

Another way to add credibility is to add examples to illustrate your points. Examples are especially effective in converting general statements into understandable and practical information. For instance, instead of saying "We are working to care for the environment," say "We are recycling plastics, glass, aluminum, and paper in our efforts to care for the environment." The former sentence is general, the latter is specific.

Jed, a financial analyst, has to present a monthly report to senior executives at his automotive supply company. "It's tempting to make sweeping statements to summarize the financial picture, but I've learned that doing so only frustrates the executives and makes me look unprepared. I now always include examples."

Jed's handout at a recent presentation included monthly data and summary statistics, plus a one-page sheet listing trends and their impact on the company. One trend he noted was "Worldwide rubber production increased 2 percent last month. Fineguard, our major rubber supplier, expects prices to go down by 1 percent in the coming months. This price reduction will impact tires, windshield wipers, and gaskets."

Jed added, "I used to report just the facts. By adding the examples of where the savings will be felt—in which products, produced by which suppliers—I help the executives see the strategic implications of the facts.

It's not that they don't know the strategic implications themselves; my report merely provides a shortcut for them."

Note that it's also a way for Jed to appropriately signal that he, too, understands the strategic implications of his analysis. Not only does adding specificity increase reader interest and enhance credibility, it boosts the writer's reputation as an expert.

EXERCISE 12: *Add Examples to Make Dull Copy Come Alive*
Shelley, a high school teacher, intends to distribute a brief explanation of how she will be calculating grades to her students. Think back to your years in school, and recall the various ways your teachers assessed your performance. Take Shelley's first draft and revise it to add specificity through numbers and examples that illustrate her points.

To: All Students

Your grade this year will be calculated based on your overall improvement. I will use a variety of tools to assess whether you understand the material. All measures are important, and I will look for your successful completion of all of them.

There are many ways this message could be revised to add specificity. Here's one good alternative. Compare the decisions you made with Shelley's second draft:

To: All Students

Your grade this year will be calculated based on your overall improvement. I will use four measures to assess how well you understand the material. All four are important. Each will count toward 25 percent of your grade. They are:

1. participation in class discussions
2. pop quizzes
3. tests
4. reports

Note how the revised version lists the four measures and describes how the total grade will be calculated. Shelley's former draft was nonspecific and vague.

How did your revision compare?

EXERCISE 13: *Add Specificity to Increase Reader Understanding*
Van, vice president of a finance company, needed to send an E-mail to alert managers that budget cuts were going to be instituted. Read Van's opening sentence below and revise it by adding specific facts, numbers, or examples to improve clarity and increase credibility. Use your imagination to make up relevant specifics, then compare your revision to the three alternatives that Van came up with.

Van's E-mail began, "In anticipation of a financial slowdown, every manager is expected to develop contingency plans."

How did you revise the sentence? Here are Van's alternatives:

1. In anticipation of a financial slowdown, every manager is expected to decide how he or she will reduce costs by 10 percent.
2. In anticipation of a financial slowdown, every manager is expected to consider ways to reduce employee travel, telecommunications, and office supply expenses.
3. In anticipation of a financial slowdown, every manager is expected to consider ways to reduce employee travel, telecommunications, and office supply expenses by 10 percent.

All three sentences are well written. Note that the first sentence adds a number (10 percent), the second one uses examples (the list of expense categories), and the third uses both. The third is probably the best choice because it provides the most details; the more specific the information you offer, the better the writing.

SELECT THE BEST WORD
TO EXPRESS YOUR MEANING

It's important that you avoid clichés. Words and phrases that are trite fail to make believable points. To succeed at encouraging action, you need to find fresh ways to express yourself.

FURY is an acronym designed to assist you in selecting specific words and phrases. FURY stands for:

*F*amiliar (e.g., *sponsorship* is a better word choice than *aegis*, for example, even though it's longer)

*U*nique (i.e., technical terminology and industry jargon)

*R*ich (e.g., *pizzazz* is better than *good*)

*Y*our favorite (i.e., the goal is not to produce writing that sounds like everybody else's but rather to find your own voice and style)

In other words, the best word is the one that's most Familiar to your target readers, unless the word in question is Unique, was selected to add Richness to the text, or is Your favorite. This tool is a handy way to make decisions about which words and phrases to use. Use the principle of FURY as you write your first draft and during the revision process.

Select Words and Phrases Easily

Hannah, a self-employed weaver, explained that she sends letters to specialty gift stores asking them to consider carrying her products. "I have a lot of trouble," Hannah says, "finding new ways to say the same thing." Here's how Hannah's most recent letter began:

Dear Store Owner:

As you plan your fall inventory assortment, I invite you to add a selection of my afghans and placemat sets to your product mix. Handwoven, they are of the highest quality wool and in unique colors.

Hannah wanted to replace two terms that she thought were trite: "highest quality" and "unique."

To come up with alternatives, first use a thesaurus to identify synonyms. There are books (such as *Roget's Thesaurus*) and online systems.

In Microsoft Word, for example, pressing shift and F7 brings up the synonym finder. Highlight the word or phrase you're trying to replace and consider your options. Once you've found a synonym, you can dig deeper for other related words. By clicking on "look up," you're able to discover subtle relationships between words that may lead you to ideas that you otherwise might not have considered. When you toss a rock into still water, circles radiate out. As you move from one word to another, the relationship between the words is like this ripple effect in the water.

As you consider Hannah's list of alternatives to "highest," note that there are subtle differences in the meaning of each word. Here's the list she came up with:

- finest
- best
- most excellent
- preeminent
- astral
- stratospheric
- top-drawer
- superior
- top

Here are Hannah's alternatives to "quality":

- attribute
- character
- characteristic
- property
- trait
- grade
- degree
- class
- factor

Once you've identified your synonym options, try using the words in various combinations. For instance, Hannah could say that her textiles exhibit the *finest characteristics*. Or *superior traits*. Or that they are of *preeminent quality*.

There is no best option. Several acceptable alternatives exist. Probably *astral* isn't a good choice because when evaluated using the FURY model, it's not familiar or unique; it is rich. But it's so esoteric, it should probably be avoided. Remember, the best words are those that are most familiar to your readers.

Hannah said, "I like the word *superior*. I decided to use it in addition to *preeminent*." Here's how she revised the phrase that used to say "highest quality":

Handwoven, the wool is of superior quality, and the workmanship is preeminent.

Thinking about the word *unique*, Hannah realized that it is overused and not exactly right. "My color combinations are unusual and special. I went to a thesaurus and used my word processor's synonym finder, and here are some alternatives I came up with that better express what I mean, rather than the trite word *unique*:

- without equal
- singular
- without rival
- alone
- apart
- incomparable
- matchless
- only
- peerless
- unequaled
- unparalleled
- lone

Hannah said, "Several of the word choices fascinated me. As I thought about it, I realized that my color combinations aren't unique—no doubt there is another weaver somewhere in the world who uses the same or similar colors—but if I talk about my work in its entirety, the wool, the handiwork, the colors, and the functionality, well, my products *are* unique. Each textile I produce is a one-of-a-kind piece, and, I believe, the best available worldwide.

"Therefore, it's accurate to say that my products are *unequaled, unparalleled, matchless,* and *incomparable.* I decided all four words were familiar, none is the unique way of expressing the thought, and they are all rich, so it came down to which was my favorite. I picked *incomparable.*"

Hannah's revised paragraph reads:

Dear Store Owner:

As you plan your fall inventory assortment, I invite you to add a selection of my afghans and placemat sets to your product mix. Handwoven, each textile is one-of-a-kind and incomparable. The design, wool, colors, and workmanship are preeminent.

Focus on Verbs to Add Power to Your Writing

Ensure that your standard business communications are engaging by selecting active verbs. Verbs—action words—serve as the pivots of sentences. Selecting dynamic verbs adds energy to your writing. The principle of FURY can help you pick targeted and compelling verbs.

"I write the instruction manuals for our appliances," explains Gary, an engineer for an appliance manufacturer. "I find I say the same things over and over again. For example, one sentence might read, 'The dial on the right is for controlling the water temperature.' Boring. Dry. There ought to be a way to add some energy."

Whenever you see a form of the verb *to be* (e.g., is, are, was, were, be, being, been), consider replacing it with another word. For example, Gary could rewrite the sentence by replacing the word *is* with *controls.* The sentence would then read, "The dial on the right controls the water temperature."

If you want to see how else you might express the thought, consider other ways to express the word *control.* Synonyms for *control* include *direct, guide, set,* and *govern,* among others. Use the FURY model to evaluate your options. In this case, Gary decided to stick with *controls.* He explained, "I liked *guides* as a word choice, but I decided that *controls* is more accurate and powerful. According to the principle of FURY, all the synonyms were familiar. None was unique. I thought *govern* was rich. But I liked *control.* It's my favorite, so I went with it."

The difference that a few words and phrases make in the overall tone and character of your writing cannot be overstated. Think about the words you select, avoid clichés, and use the FURY model to guide your choices.

EXERCISE 14: *Select Words with FURY*

Use the FURY principle to select powerful words as you revise Amanda's E-mail to add some pizzazz.

Amanda, a human resources manager for a large steel manufacturer, needed to send an E-mail to supervisors informing them that performance appraisals were due by November 15.

"It's boring," she explained, "and I couldn't think of how to add a little pep to such an ordinary business communication."

Here's Amanda's original E-mail:

To all supervisors:

All performance appraisals are due by Nov. 15. If you have any questions about how to fill out the forms or do the in-person component of the appraisal, you should read the FAQ section on the company intranet.

Amanda, ext. xxxx

Which word or words would you identify as boring? What synonyms can you list? Revise the E-mail to add some excitement.

Amanda said, "I decided to see if I could replace three words and phrases: fill out, do, and read. I went to the word-finder tool on my computer and came up with what I think were terrific replacements for them. It's amazing to me how simply changing a couple of words results in such improvement. And it was easy to do!"

Here's Amanda's revised E-mail:

To all supervisors:

All performance appraisals are due by Nov. 15. If you have any questions about how to complete the forms or conduct the in-person component of the appraisal, you should consult the FAQ section on the company intranet.

Amanda, ext. xxxx

What's your assessment of Amanda's revision? Is *complete* a better choice than *fill out*? How about *conduct* instead of *do*? Is *consult* stronger than *read*? Notice that Amanda's original words were fine; most people, however, think that her revision is better.

EXERCISE 15: *Revise in a Methodical Manner*

In the following first draft of an E-mail to retail sales staff, Les, the merchandising manager of a one-hour eyeglasses store chain, wants to institute a policy that the in-store sales staff shouldn't leave eyeglass frames scattered on the counter. Les explained that he struggled with how to word the E-mail. "I didn't want to issue an edict," he explained. "I wanted to position it as a sales strategy."

Read Les's first draft, answer the questions, and then revise the E-mail, addressing the issues raised.

Hi Sales Team:

Leaving eyeglass frames scattered over the counter looks chaotic and unappealing to customers entering our stores. It also creates confusion in customers who are trying on frames, making it hard for them to make a choice.

   Effective immediately, please ensure that frames aren't left haphazardly on the counter.

   Thanks for your cooperation.

Best, Les

What do you think? Let's take an analytical approach to evaluating Les's E-mail. To do so, we'll use the step-by-step model we've discussed thus far.

1. Is Les's objective clear? Write it out.

What did you come up with? Most of us would conclude that Les's objective is clear—sort of. We know what he *doesn't* want: glasses left scattered on the counter. What could be clearer is what he *does* want. For example, maybe Les wants the frames lined up neatly on a black velvet display pillow.

2. What do you know about his audience?

It seems clear that he is writing to Producers: matter-of-fact and bottom-line oriented. Is this smart? Of course, you can't know the personalities of all members of his sales team, but what would you speculate? What personality traits would you expect successful retail sales people to possess?

Do you think he's right to focus on Producers? Many people think he is but would aim to include some words that would appeal to other personality types, too.

3. Is the E-mail written at the proper level of formality? Complete the Formality Index.

Les knows the sales team well, although he doesn't know them all personally (perhaps a score of four is appropriate); he says that he considers them as equals in rank (a three); and he is asking them to take on extra work—definitely not good news, but not terrible news either (a three, perhaps). The score totals ten, slightly more informal than a standard business communication. Does the tone of the E-mail match this standard, and thus seem appropriate, or do you think it's a bit formal?

4. Which quadrant of the Matrix of Persuasion is he targeting?

Les seems to be assuming his writing task is Easy—that people are on his side and can do what he's asking. Therefore, he is writing only the facts. But when you think about it, Les is giving the sales staff more work. They're going to have to take the initiative to keep the counters tidy. In other words, perhaps they're not on his side, and his task is, in fact, Persuasive, not Easy.

In rereading his E-mail, you notice that while Les identifies the problem (i.e., scattered frames make the counter look chaotic) and solves the problem (i.e., don't leave frames scattered about), he doesn't explain the benefit of doing what he asks (i.e., a lack of scattered frames helps create a clean look that's proven to appeal to customers). As you'll recall from our earlier discussion about the Matrix of Persuasion, when your writing task is to persuade, you need to add benefits.

5. Which organizational structure did Les choose?

Les has not written with a clear organizational structure; this lack is a weakness in the E-mail. The E-mail uses sort of a category organizational structure; it also uses sort of a PAR organizational structure; but neither organizational structure is complete. Which organizational structure do think would be best to use?

Most people would select a PAR organizational structure, although alternatives could be effectively employed.

6. What's the Empathy Index score?

In the analysis that follows, references to the sales team (them) are in boldface; references to Les and the company (us) are underlined.

Hi **Sales Team**:

Leaving eyeglass frames scattered over the counter looks chaotic and unappealing to customers entering <u>our stores</u>. It also creates confusion in customers who are trying on frames, making it hard for them to make a choice.

Effective immediately, **please ensure** that frames aren't left haphazardly on the counter.

Thanks for **your** cooperation.

Best, <u>Les</u>

Them	4
Us	<u>(2)</u>
Empathy Index	2

A positive two is a good score. Although it could be even stronger, Les did a fine job of maintaining a reader focus in his first draft.

7. How are the lead and salutation?

Les jumps in with a key point; the lead is strong. The salutation is a clear expression of shared interest.

8. How's the close?

The sentence that begins, "Effective immediately" is aggressive and has a punitive tone. Stressing the team's cooperation might be a better approach.

9. Is it specific?

No. There are no numbers or statistics (e.g., what percentage of incoming customers find scattered frames off-putting?). Neither are there examples that would help the sales team understand what to do with the frames while customers are making their purchase decisions by comparing different frames (e.g., line up the frames on a black velvet pillow).

10. Did Les use the right words? Are the words familiar to you, unless they're unique or were selected to add richness?

Les selected some interesting words (chaotic, confusion, scattered, and unappealing, for example). They're familiar and rich. There are no unique terms used. All in all, the word choices seem appropriate, although there is a negative, almost scolding tone.

Think about what we just determined by taking this methodical approach to evaluating Les's E-mail. You want to revise it with the following points in mind:

- You need to clarify the objective and ensure that it's positive.
- You might want to broaden the audience references to include other personality types.

- You need to add more benefits to persuade your readers.
- You need to select an organizational structure.
- You need to write a less intimidating close.

Go ahead and revise Les's E-mail.

Here's how Les revised his E-mail:

Hi Sales Team:

According to our latest customer survey, over 30 percent of customers report feeling overwhelmed by their frame options. We want customers to feel confident that their decision is easy; we don't want them feeling overwhelmed. Anything we can do to assist customers in making quick and confident decisions will increase sales and customer retention.

One strategy we can all implement is to avoid leaving eyeglass frames scattered over the counter. Scattered frames seem to create confusion in customers who are trying on frames, making it harder for them to make a choice. It also looks chaotic, even intimidating, to customers entering the store.

You'll create a more comfortable and relaxed environment for your customers by keeping frames organized. Instead of allowing the frames to be haphazardly scattered on the counter, either line them up neatly or arrange them on one of the black velvet pillows available for this purpose.

Any other ideas about managing the display of frames under customer consideration? E-mail me with your best suggestions, and I'll pass them on to the entire team.

Best, Les

Notice that Les's revision is much more positive and detailed than his first draft. "I took about five minutes to analyze my first draft. That small amount of time allowed me to identify specific problems. Keeping them in mind made the revision process easier."

In this chapter, you learned two tools to improve your first drafts. You were able to add specificity by integrating numbers, facts, statistics, and examples, and you discovered how to select words and phrases using the principle of FURY as a guide. In the next chapter, you're going to learn five important strategies for ensuring that even your most complex communications emphasize your key points concisely.

Chapter Five

Revise for Impact and Clarity

CONCISE COMMUNICATIONS SUCCEED

In the last chapter you learned how to use two tools to revise your first drafts. By adding specificity with numbers, facts, statistics, and examples, you increased your communications' credibility and your readers' comprehension. By using the FURY principle, you selected the most appropriate words and phrases for your communications when you determined whether your choices were Familiar or Unique, if they would add Richness, or if they were Your favorites.

In this chapter we discuss four surefire tactics to improve your writing and learn easy-to-remember techniques to implement them. Discovering how to recognize that your communications will be improved by these four tactics will help you avoid extra revision; understanding how to correct flaws when they occur will help you polish your communications quickly and easily.

The four tactics help ensure that your writing is:

1. concise
2. clear
3. positive
4. parallel

TACTIC ONE: CONCISENESS

Ben Franklin once wrote, "Never use a longer word when a shorter word will do." Brevity is a virtue in business writing. Impatient executives, time-strapped managers, and overloaded workers want you to get to the point. But effective business writing requires more than brevity; it requires clear messages delivered in an unambiguous style.

The first tactic, conciseness, demands that you write succinctly. The need to address this issue occurs when a communication contains more words than it needs to convey your meaning. Note that length is not the issue. Rather, the issue is whether the communication has more words than are needed to transmit your message. Certainly overly long sentences are cumbersome and hard to read. Your goal, in business writing, is to aid your readers in getting your points accurately and quickly. Anything that hinders that goal is a flaw in writing.

Consider the two ways writers make their communications too wordy:

1. Sentences are too long.
2. There is too much information included in one sentence.

By examining these two causes of wordiness, you'll learn to quickly recognize and fix it in your own writing.

Keep Your Sentences Short

One reason that your writing may be too wordy is that your sentences are too long. Your sentences, on average, should contain fewer than fifteen to twenty words. For example, there's nothing wrong with a thirty-word sentence, as long as you have a six-word sentence in the same paragraph to balance it (i.e., thirty plus six divided by two equals an acceptable average sentence length of eighteen). Separating long sentences into shorter ones often adds impact.

Divide Compound Sentences to Improve Readability

One easy way to fix overly long sentences is to break them into two or more separate units. This fix works easily with compound sentences. A compound sentence is made up of two or more independent clauses—sentences—connected with a conjunction. Eliminate the connector, and you're left with two shorter sentences. Consider, for example, this sentence:

We received notice of your intention to attend the trade show, and we will send you full details by the end of the week.

The sentence is clear and straightforward but long. It has twenty-four words. Notice the word *and*. The conjunction *and* connects what could be two sentences. The sentence can be easily rewritten as:

We received notice of your intention to attend the trade show. We will send you full details by the end of the week.

The seven conjunctions you're most likely to use to connect independent clauses are *but, or, yet, so, for, and,* and *nor.* If you take the first letter of each of these seven conjunctions, you'll create the easy-to-remember acronym BOY'S FAN. Finding one of these seven words used in this way—to connect two independent clauses to form one long sentence—allows you to quickly fix an overly long sentence.

Review the following examples. In each example, you'll see the pattern of compound sentences and learn how to separate them into two sentences, if you decide to do so.

Before: The Acme Corporation quote to update the manufacturing facility's computer system exceeded both our capital and operating budget limits, but we decided to accept it anyway because their service guarantee is the best. (thirty-three words)

After: The Acme Corporation quote to update the manufacturing facility's computer system exceeded both our capital and operating budget limits. We decided to accept it anyway because their service guarantee is the best. (Two sentences of nineteen and thirteen words averages sixteen words per sentence.)

Before: After reviewing landscaping and engineering concerns, we will build on the location farthest from the river, or if that location is deemed unacceptable, we may hire a surveyor to review other building site alternatives. (thirty-four words)

After: After reviewing landscaping and engineering concerns, we will build on the location farthest from the river. If that location is deemed unacceptable, we may hire a surveyor to review other building site alternatives. (Two sentences of sixteen and seventeen words averages sixteen-and-a-half words per sentence.)

Before: By hiring an on-site nurse, we expect to reduce some employee absences, so after reviewing the attached draft of the job description, let's schedule a time to discuss how best to implement this plan. (thirty-four words)

After: By hiring an on-site nurse, we expect to reduce some employee absences. After reviewing the attached draft of the job description, let's schedule a time to discuss how best to implement this plan. (Two sentences of twelve and twenty-one words averages sixteen-and-a-half words per sentence.)

Anytime you see this pattern, a sentence composed of two complete thoughts connected by one of the BOY'S FAN words, consider breaking it into two sentences.

Find Comfortable Break Points to Shorten Complicated Sentences

Another reason sentences can be difficult to follow is that they're long and complicated. Whereas compound sentences include two independent clauses connected by a BOY'S FAN word, complicated sentences follow a different pattern.

Typically, a long, complicated sentence starts with a logical structure: It begins with the subject, followed by the verb that goes with the subject, then the object. (The subject is the doer of the action implied by the verb and the object is the receiver of this action.) After this promising beginning, the writer of a complicated sentence usually adds a series of prepositional phrases. Each prepositional phrase might impart important information. Taken together, however, they add too much information all at once. The net result is that the readers aren't informed—they're confused.

Complicated sentences can be shortened by separating units of information. Consider, for example, the following forty-word sentence:

I have reviewed your letter of complaint explaining the difficulties you had in registering your company's representatives for the National Widget Conference and Trade Show on our website, which was unexpectedly down since our Internet service provider guarantees access.

Most of us would agree that this sentence is poorly written; the writer never apologizes to the customer, for example. Also, it's too long, too wordy, and the writer's purpose is unclear. To start revising it, look for a BOY'S FAN word. Not there. Thus you know the problem isn't that the sentence is compound. It's complicated. It starts simply enough with a traditional structure of subject/verb/object:

I have reviewed your letter.

If you chose, you could stop there. Note that the sentence continues with a series of prepositional and other phrases:

of complaint
explaining the difficulties you had
in registering your company's representatives
for the National Widget Conference and Trade Show
on our website,
which was unexpectedly down
since our Internet service provider guarantees access.

You could revise the sentence to end at the conclusion of any one of these phrases. For example, you might revise the sentence to read:

I have reviewed your letter of complaint. *(seven words)*

Or, you might end here:

I have reviewed your letter of complaint explaining the difficulties you had. *(twelve words)*

Or here:

I have reviewed your letter of complaint explaining the difficulties you had in registering your company's representatives. *(seventeen words)*

Or here:

I have reviewed your letter of complaint explaining the difficulties you had in registering your company's representatives for the National Widget Conference and Trade Show. *(twenty-five words)*

Or even here:

I have reviewed your letter of complaint explaining the difficulties you had in registering your company's representatives for the National Widget Conference and Trade Show on our website. *(twenty-nine words)*

There's no one best place to end the sentence. It's your choice. Once you've made your decision, you can easily revise the remaining phrase so it also becomes a complete sentence. For example, you might write:

Please accept my apology that our website was down.

Consider this revision option:

I have reviewed your letter of complaint explaining the difficulties you had in registering your company's representatives for the National Widget Conference and Trade Show. Please accept my apology that our website was down. *(Two sentences of twenty-five and ten words average seventeen-and-a-half words per sentence.)*

Isn't it better? When revising a complicated sentence, look for a subject/verb/object construction followed by a series of phrases. Find comfortable stopping places, and revise the beginning of each additional sentence to include all appropriate information in the form of a subject, verb, and object.

No matter how long or short your sentences are, you need to avoid sentence fragments. A sentence fragment cannot stand alone as a sentence. (Note that exclamatory expressions such as "Wow!," "Terrific presentation!," or "Too bad!" represent complete sentences.)

A fragment usually lacks words from an adjacent sentence that it needs in order to become complete. Whether the words are nearby, or simply missing, be certain that every sentence has a subject (the doer of the action) and a verb that goes with the subject, and that every sentence expresses a complete thought.

EXERCISE 16: *Revise for Conciseness*

Gloria, an administrative assistant in a silk flower company, said, "My boss sends out proposals to hotel executives. Her ideas are good, but she's wordy. I always have to revise her writing, but it's important that I preserve her meaning."

Read the following paragraph from one of the proposals Gloria needs to revise, and rewrite it so that it's clear, focused, and appropriately short.

> As the leader in the silk flower industry, we create arrangements that are lush and full and always custom designed, featuring seasonal blossoms in an array of colors to create just the look you seek whether the occasion is a wedding, reunion, business meeting or conference, or other event. We guarantee that every arrangement will be designed to your specifications, and we promise that our custom designs will be delivered on time and at or below budget. *(Two sentences of forty-nine and twenty-eight words average thirty-eight-and-a-half words per sentence—too long.)*

How did you approach this exercise? Did you first look to see if one of the two sentences was a compound sentence? Often, that's the easiest way to begin revising long or complicated sentences.

In this example, the second sentence is compound; two independent clauses are connected with the BOY'S FAN word *and*. Breaking the clauses into two separate units might be a good start to the revision.

> We guarantee that every arrangement will be designed to your specifications. We promise that our custom designs will be delivered on time and at or below budget. *(Two sentences of eleven and sixteen words average thirteen-and-a-half words per sentence.)*

Note that each sentence is stronger than was the one, longer sentence. Now that you see them one after another, however, do you notice the redundant structure? The first begins, "We guarantee." The second begins, "We promise." Given the similarity, it might be better to combine them.

> We guarantee that every arrangement will be custom designed to your specifications, delivered on time, and at or below budget. *(twenty words)*

Can you hear how much more powerful this one sentence is?

What about the first sentence? Note that it's not compound; it's complicated. Useful details are provided, but too much information is given all at once.

As the leader in the silk flower industry, we create arrangements that are lush and full and always custom-designed, featuring seasonal blossoms in an array of colors to create just the look you seek whether the occasion is a wedding, reunion, business meeting or conference, or other event. *(forty-nine words)*

When revising a complicated sentence, it's often a good approach to list all of the thoughts being expressed and aim to create separate sentences.

How many thoughts are expressed in this example? Four: the look of the flowers, the custom preparation, the contents of the arrangements, and the occasions the company serves.

Most people, in revising this sentence, combine the first two thoughts and write a twenty-word sentence, as follows:

As the leader in the silk flower industry, we create arrangements that are lush and full and always custom designed.

You could have stopped sooner, expressing only one thought. This approach would create a sixteen-word sentence:

As the leader in the silk flower industry, we create arrangements that are lush and full.

Continuing on, you could have revised the second thought expressed in the sentence as a five-word sentence:

Every arrangement is custom designed.

The next thought might be expressed as follows:

All arrangements feature seasonal blossoms in an array of colors to create just the look you seek. *(seventeen words)*

The final thought might become:

Our flowers will be perfect, whether the occasion is a wedding, reunion, business meeting or conference, or other event. *(nineteen words)*

Let's evaluate the total revision:

As the leader in the silk flower industry, we create arrangements that are lush and full and always custom designed. All arrangements feature seasonal blossoms in an array of colors to create just the look you seek. Our flowers will be perfect, whether the occasion is a wedding, reunion, business meeting or conference, or other event. We guarantee that every arrangement will be custom designed to your specifications, delivered on time, and at or below budget. *(Four sentences totaling seventy-six words [20 + 17 + 19 + 20 = 76] average nineteen words per sentence.)*

Gloria explains, "Knowing to look first for a compound sentence and then for a complicated sentence made revising much easier. I like having a model that provides specific steps."

No matter how you revised this example, ask yourself if you made it more concise. Did you shorten sentences while preserving the author's intention? Did you convey needed information?

Remember, when shortening sentences, use as many words as you need to make your points, but no more.

TACTIC TWO: CLARITY

If your readers have to study your communications to understand your message, you're slowing them down and making them work unnecessarily hard. Reader confusion often results from a lack of writer preparation. However, even when you've followed the steps outlined in this book, you might leave your readers confused because of two specific issues:

1. misplaced or misused modifiers
2. unexplained acronyms or technical jargon

Selecting and positioning modifying words and phrases correctly and defining all terminology that may be unfamiliar to your readers will help ensure clarity in your communications.

Modify Properly to Add Emphasis and Clarity

Adverbs, adjectives, and prepositional phrases are among the ways to modify words and phrases in business writing. They can add important or interesting details. But they can also be confusing.

Adverbs May Weaken Verbs

Instead of adding words and phrases that modify verbs, it's often better to select the most exact verb. Choosing an on-target verb adds impact to the sentence and may eliminate an unneeded adverb. In the following examples, note the effectiveness of choosing the precise verb.

The committee carefully considered the proposed reorganization.

The committee deliberated the proposed reorganization.

The word *deliberated* means "carefully considered."

The negotiations quickly fell apart when the partner said no.

The negotiations collapsed when the partner said no.

Note that *collapsed* means "quickly fell apart."

When you choose the most action-oriented verbs possible, you can usually avoid adding unnecessary adverbs.

Adjectives May Diminish the Impact of Your Nouns

Likewise, adjectives often diminish the power of the nouns they modify. Sometimes the modifying words or phrases distract the reader by adding unnecessary information. For example, which of these two sentences is stronger?

The hotel's computerized fire alarm system will be tested on Tuesday.

The hotel's fire alarm system will be tested on Tuesday.

The fact that the system is "computerized" may be relevant in some contexts (in an application to win an insurance reduction because of updated equipment, for instance), but to employees or guests it's probably irrelevant. It may also be confusing. What has the fact that it's computerized got to do with the fact that it will be tested on Tuesday? It's more concise to eliminate it.

Sometimes the adjective is redundant, as in this example:

The memo provides *helpful* suggestions about maximizing your new computer's capabilities.

What other kind of suggestions would you publish in a memo? Other adjective alternatives beg the same question: Are they *useful* suggestions? One hopes so. *Relevant* suggestions? They ought to be. *Valuable* suggestions? Good, but as with "helpful," why would you publish them if they weren't valuable? Better to let the noun do the work:

The memo provides suggestions about maximizing your new computer's capabilities.

Use adjectives when they're necessary to impart correct information, and avoid them when they don't. When you use adjectives, be sure to choose words that accurately express your meaning. For example, consider these two sentences:

Mary was very happy to receive a promotion.

Mary was thrilled to receive a promotion.

Thrilled means "very happy" and is a more exact and interesting choice. Words such as *very* and *good* are weak and can almost always be replaced by a more precise and engaging term.

Modifying Phrases May Confuse Your Readers
Misplaced modifying phrases sometimes result in odd, even humorous interpretations. Be certain to position the modifying word or phrase as close as possible to the term that is being modified. Consider, for example:

One of our executives has been sent to a counselor with a drinking problem.

A counselor with a drinking problem? It would be better to write:

One of our executives with a drinking problem has been sent to a counselor.

The modifying phrase "with a drinking problem" needs to be next to what is being modified—in this example, "one of our executives." How about this sentence:

This memo describes how to protect your possessions from our risk adjusters.

Thieving risk adjusters? It would be better to write:

This memo from our risk adjusters describes how to protect your possessions.

Sometimes the meaning is impossible to decipher. Read the following sentence:

The software engineer has been trying to get us to review his agreement for six weeks.

Do you see the problem? Because of the placement of the modifying phrase "for six weeks," the writer's intention is unclear. Here are three possible interpretations:

1. For six weeks, the software engineer has been trying to get us to review his agreement.

2. The software engineer has been trying to get us to review his six-week agreement.

3. The software engineer has been trying to get us to undertake a six-week review of his agreement.

Placing the modifying phrase next to the word or phrase that it is intended to modify solves this problem.

Explain Everything Unless All
Your Readers Will Understand

In Chapter One, we discussed how acronyms impact readers' perceptions about the formality or informality of your communications. Acronyms and technical terminology need to be explained, defined, or referenced unless 100 percent of your readers understand the jargon. Keep in mind that even if most of your readers know what you mean, some might not. Be sensitive to guests and newcomers. Acronyms can be useful as shorthand, but they can be confusing to readers who aren't familiar with your terminology. When in doubt, write it out.

The traditional way to handle acronyms is to write out the complete term, name, title, department, or phrase the first time it's used, and then to indicate the acronym within parentheses. Once you've followed this format, you may confidently use only the acronym thereafter. For example:

English as a Foreign Language (EFL) courses will begin on Wednesday. Tuition for all EFL courses will be reimbursed for employees who achieve a passing grade.

Instead of using parentheses, you might choose a different approach. You might use a glossary, sidebar, footnotes, or endnotes, for example, to explain or define all terminology.

Kathleen, the administrative assistant to the chief executive officer (CEO) of a physical therapy provider, decided to use a sidebar in her newsletter. "The newsletter goes to patients. 'ROM' means 'range of motion' and is a much-used term in the industry. But if you've just started working with us to get back full use of your arm, you may not be familiar with the term 'ROM.' To define it in every article, or even in every issue of the newsletter, was a pain and seemed like overkill. But I knew that some people receiving each issue wouldn't know the jargon. What I did was create a sidebar on the cover. I called it 'Jargon' and defined all the terms used in that issue. That way I didn't have to worry about it at all." Titling the glossary "Jargon" is a nice touch; it lets readers know that ignorance is expected.

Successful business writing demands clarity. Make it easy, not hard, for your readers to get your message.

EXERCISE 17: *Revise to Create Proper Emphasis*
and Increase Clarity

Barry, a sales manager for a large printer, explains, "I'm always wordy. I find myself writing run-on sentences and I don't use modifiers well."

Take a look at Barry's E-mail draft asking his sales staff for their analysis of why sales are down.

> After looking thoroughly at your reports on last month's sales calls describing who you saw and what objections to closing the sales were raised, and reviewing those special and extraordinary events such as the blizzard in the upper Midwest, as well as standard events such as President's Day, there seems to be no clear or definitive reason why sales are down. In anticipation of our next regular meeting, I would like to solicit your good ideas about what's going wrong and what we all and each of us can do to impact it. *(Two sentences of sixty-one and thirty-two words average forty-six-and-a-half words.)*

You'll note that Barry's E-mail is long and unclear. You'll also note many modifying words and phrases. As you work to revise it, follow the steps that have been outlined thus far in this chapter:

1. Look for compound sentences. If you find one, consider breaking the sentence into two or more separate units.
2. In complicated sentences, consider how many separate thoughts and ideas are being expressed. Can any be eliminated? Are any redundant? Can separate thoughts be written as separate sentences?
3. Think about Barry's use of adverbs, adjectives, and modifying phrases. Are they needed? Or are they diminishing the impact of his verbs and nouns, and thus should be eliminated?
4. Decide if the ideas expressed in the modifying phrases are important. If they are, are there more precise words that can substitute for the longer phrases?

How did you do? Following the steps above, start by looking for compound sentences. Are there any coordinating conjunctions (one of the BOY'S FAN words)? No, there aren't.

Next, list separate thoughts being expressed in each sentence. The first sentence:

> After looking thoroughly at your reports on last month's sales calls describing who you saw and what objections to closing the sales were raised, and reviewing those special and extraordinary events such as the blizzard in the upper Midwest, as well as standard events such as President's Day, there seems to be no clear or definitive reason why sales are down.

The thoughts and ideas expressed are:

1. I've looked at your reports.
2. I've read whom you called on and why they said no deal.
3. I've considered whether special events such as blizzards would account for weak sales.
4. I've considered whether the shortened work month (because of the President's Day holiday) would account for the weak sales.
5. I can't understand why sales are down.

Five separate points, all independent and necessary, are a lot to integrate into one sentence.

In the second sentence, there were three separate thoughts expressed:

> In anticipation of our next regular meeting, I would like to solicit your good ideas about what's going wrong and what we all and each of us can do to impact it.

1. I'm getting ready for our next sales meeting.
2. I want to know what you think the problem is.
3. I want to know what you think we can do to fix the problem.

We now have a total of eight thoughts to express. Were there any redundancies? Did you select more precise words? Eliminating redundancies and evaluating modifiers makes shortening and separating thoughts and ideas easier.

There are many good ways to concisely communicate those eight thoughts. Barry decided to focus on his bottom-line objective. "I wanted them to submit ideas by Tuesday, before the meeting," he explained.

Read Barry's revision and then his comments:

> After scrutinizing last months' sales reports, the reasons for the downturn remain unclear. Even after considering events such as the blizzard in the upper Midwest and the President's Day holiday, there seems to be no definitive reason why sales are down. What do you think is the problem? What should we do differently? Please E-mail me your ideas by Tuesday, and I'll present them at the next sales meeting. *(Five sentences totaling sixty-nine words [13 + 28 + 7 + 5 + 16 = 69] average just under fourteen words per sentence.)*

"I decided to get rid of the junk and focus on the key points. Taking my draft and listing the ideas I wanted to express was great! After I did that, I focused on tightening up modifiers like 'looking thoroughly.' That means 'scrutinizing,' so I said 'scrutinizing.' Overall, I was pleased with my final revision. It was simpler, more focused on my objective, and much clearer."

TACTIC THREE: A POSITIVE TONE

Negative words and phrases such as "not," "you don't," "you're not able to," and the like should rarely be used. If you use such terminology frequently, you dilute the impact of the words. If, on the other hand, you use them judiciously, you underscore your point, adding emphasis and urgency to your communications.

People don't like to read or respond to bad news. In Chapter Two, we reviewed organizational structures that help you say no or deliver bad news as smoothly as possible. Now let's examine negative words and phrases themselves and see if you can select alternatives that will more effectively generate the results you seek.

Choose the Positive Over the Negative

Highlight good news instead of bad news by writing about what can occur, not what can't. Consider the following two sentences:

He can't see you until four.
He can see you at four.

One is negative, the other positive. It makes good business sense to write with a positive, not a negative, focus. For instance:

The legislation prohibits most transactions.
The legislation permits some transactions.

While you want to make your points clearly and honestly, you want to maintain as positive a tone as you can.

TACTIC FOUR:
PARALLEL CONSTRUCTION

Adhering to the principles of parallel construction facilitates readers' comprehension of your messages, reduces your writing and revision effort, creates a pleasing rhythm to the writing, and adds professionalism to your communications. You should adhere to the decisions you make consistently throughout a document, and often throughout all of the documents produced within an organization.

Some examples of parallel construction issues are:

- grammatical constructions
- titles, names, and honorifics
- sentence or clause structure within a bulleted or numbered list
- modifying phrases
- punctuation styles
- nouns and pronouns

Construct Consistent Lists

Creating a list is an easy way to maintain parallel construction. In any listing of items or activities, whether it's narrative or uses graphics such as bullet points or numbering, maintain the same tense and grammatical organization from one unit of information to the next.

Narrative Lists

It's important to use the same verb tense within a list. Consider the following sentence, for example:

Applicants will be interviewed, tested, and after the interview they can ask questions.

Notice the first two verbs are in the past tense: interviewed and tested. The last verb, however, is constructed differently: can ask. It would be better to maintain the same grammatical construction throughout:

Applicants will be interviewed, tested, and invited to ask questions.

Consider this sentence:

The job description must be rewritten, we must advertise the position, and interviews must commence by the end of the week.

Adhering to the principle of parallel construction, it would be better to write:

By the end of the week, we must rewrite the job description, advertise the position, and begin interviewing.

Note a similar issue in the following sentence: The beginning is constructed differently from the end.

Customers rely on our design and engineering expertise, and we're able to build and landscape, too.

It would be better to write:

Customers rely on our expertise in designing, engineering, building, and landscaping.

Bulleted Lists

Bulleted lists organize information and help your readers scan quickly. In such lists, it's important to start each bullet with the same part of speech.

Notice the following two lists are both properly constructed, although they're different from one another. Both lists explain the updates currently being installed on a company's website.

Option One
Once the update is completed, visitors to our website will be able to:

- search for past articles from the newsletters
- contact any employee by E-mail
- consult frequently asked questions
- link to other sites

Option Two
Once the update is completed, visitors to our website will be able to access information in new ways:

- Customers will be able to search through the archive of past newsletter issues to find articles of specific or immediate interest.
- Prospects will be able to directly contact any employee by name, department, or activity.
- Users of our products will be able to consult frequently asked questions twenty-four hours a day.
- Interested surfers can link directly to other sites.

Note that in option one, each bullet point started with a verb, whereas option two used complete sentences. They're both effective. Pick one, or create your own style, then be consistent.

Duane, executive director of a museum, needed to write a list of goals to present to the board of directors. He wrote:

- to attract more volunteers
- ask for an increase in member dues
- considering adding exhibitions
- to increase the number of grants we receive
- interview new artists and publishing the interviews in the newsletter

Duane said, "As soon as I read through the list, I knew I had a problem. Not just with parallel construction. Some of my writing was unclear because, frankly, I wasn't sure what I wanted to say. I decided to go one by one, getting each bullet point into parallel construction and making sure the points were clear. There were a lot of verbs close to the beginning, so I decided to stay with that construction. I ended up with this.

My goals include:

- to attract more volunteers
- to analyze whether an increase in member dues is appropriate
- to consider adding exhibitions
- to receive more grants
- to conduct and publish interviews with new artists

"I was very pleased with the outcome. Once I got into the rhythm of it, the list wrote itself."

Watch *Either* and *Neither*

In sentences that use *either/or* and *neither/nor*, keep two-word verbs together and be certain that the verb comes before *either* or *neither*. For example:

We have neither reviewed the report nor the videotape.

You need to keep the verb *have reviewed* together and write:

We have reviewed neither the report nor the videotape.

Similarly, "You may either select Mary or Jason" should be written as "You may select either Mary or Jason."

Be Certain Titles and Names Are Consistent

Be vigilant in maintaining parallel construction in your use of titles and names. For instance, if you refer to the chairman of the board as "Mr. Jones," you should refer to everyone by their title and last name, from the janitor to the secretaries, from long-term senior executives to new entry-level employees.

Likewise, if you refer to someone whose title is "Dr.," maintain parallel construction in referring to any other people in the same communication. For instance, if you write about Dr. Smith, then you should refer to all of the doctor's staff by title and last name, too (e.g., Ms. Smith and Mr. Brown, not Mary and Charlie).

Adhering to the principle of parallel construction helps your readers understand your meaning, saves you writing time, and enhances your professional image.

EXERCISE 18: *Write a Third Draft*

In the following example, Stuart, an analyst for a city government agency, has followed the steps outlined in the book thus far. "My boss told me it is imperative that I be precise in my writing," explains Stuart, "and I agree. She needed a report about school renovations. I want the report to be clear and straightforward.

"My objective is to arm my boss with plenty of facts and figures for her next town hall meeting. She's a top adviser to the mayor, so she appears with him often and needs to be able to field questions and feed him facts. She's completely a Producer, so I try to use a lot of lists and graphs to help her get the information she needs quickly. She's on my side and has the resources she needs to do the job, so it's an Easy writing assignment. The report needs to be quite formal, because it's part of the public record. I selected the PAR organizational structure to focus on the bottom line, which I knew would make the report most user-friendly to my boss.

"I wrote it and used the Empathy Index and principle of FURY to revise it. Now I'm ready to finish it up."

An introduction in a report or proposal typically presents an overview of what's to come, piquing readers' interest. As you'll see, Stuart's introduction does a good job of setting the scene and providing a big-picture synopsis. However, it suffers from several flaws. After you read the following paragraph from Stuart's second draft, you'll find instructions. Here's Stuart's draft:

With last year's budget cuts integrated throughout the agency, we've been tracking their effects on our performance in several key areas including repair of streets and fixing potholes, snow removal, trash collection,

115

collecting goods for recycling, including updating guard railings on highways, and we can demonstrate and show that turnaround time from initial
complaint or report receiving to ultimate repair, replacement, or adjusting
it has taken 23 percent longer, on average. While we all, every one of us,
have risen to the challenge of providing the citizens of this great city excellent service, this is unacceptable, as I'm sure you'll agree.

Revise Stuart's introduction by following the steps that have been outlined in this chapter:

1. Look for compound sentences. If you find one, consider breaking
   the sentence into two or more separate units.
2. In complicated sentences, consider how many separate thoughts
   and ideas are being expressed. Can any be eliminated? Are
   any redundant? Can separate thoughts be written as separate
   sentences?
3. Think about Stuart's use of adverbs, adjectives, and modifying
   phrases. Are they needed? Or are they diminishing the impact of
   his verbs and nouns, and thus should be eliminated?
4. If ideas expressed in the modifying phrases are important, are
   there more precise words you can substitute for longer phrases?
5. Is parallel construction maintained throughout?

Rewrite Stuart's paragraph with an eye to increasing its clarity and
simplicity while preserving the meaning and tone.

How did you do? Compare your thinking to Stuart's as you review his
comments and revision.

1. Look for compound sentences. If you find one, consider breaking
   the sentence into two or more separate units.

"I realized that the first sentence was way too long. Seventy-one words.
Wow. It was compound and complicated. The first thing I did was break
it into two separate units."

With last year's budget cuts integrated throughout the agency, we've
been tracking their effects on our performance in several key areas
including repair of streets and fixing potholes, snow removal, trash col-

lection, collecting goods for recycling, including updating guard railings on highways. We can demonstrate and show that turnaround time from initial complaint or report receiving to ultimate repair, replacement, or adjusting it has taken 23 percent longer, on average.

"When I divided it, I got two sentences, one forty-two words long, the other twenty-eight words long. Still too long. The original second sentence was thirty words long. But it's not a compound sentence."

2. In complicated sentences, consider how many separate thoughts and ideas are being expressed. Can any be eliminated? Are any redundant? Can separate thoughts be written as separate sentences?

"I decided to separate all thoughts in the entire paragraph as a tool to help me make the introduction more concise. Here are the thoughts I want to express."

1. Last year's budget cuts have been integrated into this year's activities.
2. They've affected our performance.
3. We are responsible for:

   - repair of streets
   - repair of potholes
   - snow removal
   - trash collection
   - recycled goods collection
   - repair of highway guard railings

4. Our response record has suffered, dropping 23 percent since the budget cuts were initiated.
5. We're trying to do the best we can.
6. We need to do better.
7. We believe that you, the citizens, think we need to do better.
8. We hope you will agree to a tax increase so that we can have adequate funds to provide the level of service you want.

"I realized that I'd skipped the last thought completely—on purpose. Requesting an increase in taxes is where we're heading, but we're not there yet. And it's not my place to write about it. It's not even my boss's place. It's her boss's job—the mayor's.

"In any event, I identified eight separate thoughts. That's a lot of thoughts to include in two, or even three, sentences. Plus the sentences are still too long. What I did as my first stab was to add bullets, because I know my boss likes them."

With last year's budget cuts integrated throughout the agency, we've been tracking their effects on our performance in several key areas, including:

- repair of streets and fixing potholes
- snow removal
- trash collection
- collecting goods for recycling
- updating guard railings on highways

We can demonstrate and show that turnaround time from initial complaint or report receiving to ultimate repair, replacement, or adjusting it has taken 23 percent longer, on average. While we all, every one of us, have risen to the challenge of providing the citizens of this great city excellent service, this is unacceptable as I'm sure you'll agree.

3. Think about Stuart's use of adverbs, adjectives, and modifying phrases. Are they needed? Or are they diminishing the impact of his verbs and nouns, and thus should be eliminated?
4. If the ideas expressed in the modifying phrases are important, are there more precise words that can substitute for his longer phrases?
5. Is parallel construction maintained throughout?

"I looked at these three steps together. I had lots of redundancies and misused modifiers. Plus, I had parallel construction problems. I went phrase by phrase. Here's my next version."

With last year's budget cuts fully integrated, we've noted an effect on our performance in several key areas:

- repair of streets and potholes
- removal of snow
- collection of trash
- collection of recyclable goods
- repair of highway guard railings

The turnaround time from first report to completed repair has taken, on average, 23 percent longer than it did last year.

"I cut the entire last sentence. I didn't need it. The more I kept my focus on my objective, the better my writing got."

Notice how Stuart eliminated repetitive words and phrases, aligned construction to ensure a parallel structure, and simplified the content.

What do you think? Is it clearer? Certainly it's shorter. What's your view? Is it more reader friendly? Is it more usable by Stuart's boss at a town meeting?

Most people agree that it is better. Stuart applied the principles we've discussed in a methodical manner, and his writing improved. "Plus," he explained, "I learned to write keeping parallel construction and avoiding redundancy in mind. By writing cleaner communications in the first place, I speeded up the entire process."

When you begin to write with the four tactics in mind, it will take you less time to produce better communications, and your efforts are more likely to succeed.

In this chapter, you've learned how to write concisely and clearly, add a positive tone, and maintain parallel construction. You've seen how assimilating tips to avoid these pitfalls helps you write tighter, more readable initial drafts.

Whether you wrote with these four tactics in mind, or revised to apply them, your communications are close to complete. You're ready to confirm that your grammar and punctuation are correct.

In the next chapter, you're going to learn to decide what level of proofreading is appropriate for you and your projects in advance, and you'll use specific proofreading techniques to quickly and easily find grammar and punctuation errors.

CHAPTER SIX

Determine What Kind of Proofing You Require

INTEGRATE PROOFING INTO THE WRITING PROCESS

In the last chapter, you learned four easy-to-use tactics to improve your writing. You discovered how to achieve conciseness, enhance clarity, establish a positive tone, and maintain parallel construction.

In this chapter, we're going to look at the level of proofreading that is appropriate for your projects and discuss the types of errors, omissions, and inconsistencies for which you'll need to proof. You'll also be alerted to the most common grammatical and punctuation errors found in business writing.

UNDERSTAND PROOFREADING'S ROLE IN THE BUSINESS WRITING PROCESS

Proofreading is a key part of producing effective business communications and needs to be integrated into the writing process. Many people think that proofreading occurs once, at the end of the writing process. In fact, most professional writers proofread early and often, knowing that they'll save their organizations time and money if they catch and correct errors promptly.

The Rule of Five demonstrates the point that the earlier you catch an error, the less time and money it will take to fix the mistake. While the specific numbers aren't the issue, the dollar amounts quoted below are reasonable guesstimates, and it's the relative relationship of the numbers that makes the point. Note that the cost of correcting an error increases geometrically, rising sharply the longer it takes to identify the problem.

An error caught on the computer monitor, for example, before anything's been printed, costs your company about $5. If the error is caught once the document has been printed, fixing it costs your company about $50. If the document has been sent to a commercial printer and film has been created before the error is caught, correcting it costs the company close to $500.

And if the item has been printed, the error costs a minimum of $5,000 to fix.

Proofing as you write, and at every step of the revision process, helps you catch errors earlier rather than later.

DETERMINE YOUR EDITING LEVEL BEFORE YOU BEGIN TO PROOF

Editing is strenuous work. It's always detail-oriented and often time-consuming. But not all writing projects require comprehensive editing. Sometimes your message is simple to express. Simple communications can often be proofed quickly. However, if the communication is complex—a report or proposal, for instance—comprising multiple sections that need to be evaluated individually and as a whole, proofreading is likely to be a demanding task.

As a general statement, the more complicated the communication, the more careful the proofing that's required. It's important to decide which of the following three proofing levels is appropriate for your project before you begin to proof. The three levels are:

Level One: Clarity and Grammar
Level Two: Clarity, Grammar, Organization, and Completeness
Level Three: Everything

You'll save time and energy if you don't proof beyond what is required. And you'll produce professional and polished communications if you proof as you go along.

Level One: Check Clarity and Grammar

Danielle, a graphic designer, says, "I send E-mails back and forth to other designers and to the writers within the company all day long. I want my communications to convey a professional image, but they're usually short and simple, so what's most important for me to proof is that my meaning is clear and my grammar is correct. Beyond that, proofing would be a waste of time."

Note that the first level of proofing is appropriate for Danielle because her communications have these attributes:

- internal
- short
- simple
- informal
- low risk, with only minor consequences associated with inaccuracies

Level Two: Evaluate Clarity, Grammar, Organization, and Completeness

Nancee, a self-employed makeup artist, writes sales letters, proposals, business correspondence, E-mails, and Web copy. "I hate to write!" she explains. "But in business, I have to. So I do. What I've learned over the years, though, is that people hire me for my expertise and upbeat personality, not my writing ability, or as I like to joke, my writing inability! Still, I know how important it is that I convey a highly professional image. Proofing matters a lot."

In evaluating Nancee's circumstances, it's clear that the second level of proofing is appropriate. Her projects have the following characteristics:

- external, but not part of the public record
- short to medium in length
- simple to somewhat complex
- informal
- medium risk, with relatively minor consequences associated with errors or inaccuracies

Level Three: Proof Everything—Be Methodical

There are two kinds of third-level projects: communications for which you are responsible for writing to someone else's specifications with little or no direction, and communications for which the consequences of errors are severe.

"My boss sends me E-mails with—at best—a rough draft of a message," explains Heidi, executive assistant to a consumer products company's senior vice president. "The projects range from an E-mail to all vice presidents about some policy change to a five-page proposal to another corporation's president presenting a global cobranding initiative.

"Sometimes he'll jot down a sentence or two, sometimes he'll write theoretically about what he wants to accomplish, and sometimes he'll do both at the same time. It's my job to take whatever he gives me and produce a finished document ready for his signature. We joke that my responsibility is to 'proof' his work. But we both know that this is way beyond traditional proofreading. It's really writing, editing, and proofing."

Heidi's approach to creating finished documents is an example of the third level of proofing. Her projects have the following attributes:

- external, and potentially part of the public record
- short to long
- usually complex
- usually formal
- medium to high risk, with significant consequences associated with errors or inaccuracies

Ray, a physical therapist, says that he has to write a monthly article of about five hundred words for his organization's newsletter. "Five hundred words is a lot. That's a long article compared to the rest of the newsletter. Having that amount of space allows me to go into a fair amount of detail. It's imperative that my articles be clear and accurate. Our newsletter targets people who are recovering from sports injuries. The readers are usually anxious and may not know a lot about the subject matter. Clarity is my most important goal. However, because the newsletters are distributed to the community through doctors' offices, the public library, schools, and the recreation department, they are public documents. My boss once told me that I should always write about medical subjects as though the article would end up as evidence in a court-room someday. So I'm very cautious. It's important to me personally and professionally that they be correct, grammatical, complete, and clear."

Ray's articles are another example of proofing at the third level. They have these qualities:

- external, and potentially part of the public record
- long
- complex
- formal
- high risk, with severe consequences associated with inaccuracies

Your first task is to identify which level of editing is appropriate for you. If you proof everything in every project, you'll spend needless time and effort for no or little reward. On the other hand, if you don't proof everything on certain projects, you risk costly mistakes.

Assess Your Projects One by One

In order to make smart decisions about which level of editing is appropriate for your projects, you need to know what factors to evaluate. The assessment that follows will help you determine the proper level of editing for any project.

Bring to mind a specific writing project, then assess how true or not true each of the following statements is. If the statement is absolutely true, score it a five. If the statement is absolutely false, score it a one. If it's sometimes true, sort of true, or maybe true, score it a three. A two implies that the statement is rarely true, and a four implies that the statement is usually true. At the end, tally your scores and read what your total score implies about the appropriate level of editing for your project.

1. Your communication will be distributed only within your organization. _____
2. Using the Formality Index, you've determined that your communication is very informal. _____
3. Your message is upbeat and fun. _____

4. If your readers misunderstand your message, no negative consequences will result. _____
5. Your communication is short. _____
6. Your communication is simple. _____
7. Your communication includes only one section. For example, it's
   a 100-word newsletter article, a business letter, a memo, or an
   E-mail with no attachments. _____
8. Only one subject is included in your communication. _____
9. Using the Matrix of Persuasion (see Chapter One), you've determined that your readers are on your side and that they have the
   resources to do as you ask; in other words, you've assessed your
   writing task as Easy. _____

Tally your scores. Your total will be between nine and forty-five. (If you
scored each of the nine statements as a one, your total score will be nine.
If you scored each a five, your total score will be forty-five.) The higher
your score, the lower the level of proofreading you need to undertake.

- 33 to 45 implies that it would be appropriate to proof for clarity
  and grammar (Level One)
- 20 to 32 implies that it would be appropriate to proof for clarity,
  grammar, organization, and completeness (Level Two)
- 9 to 19 implies that it would be appropriate to proof for everything (Level Three)

Use a Checklist to Confirm That Your Proofing Is Complete

Whatever level of editing you've determined is appropriate for your project, use the checklists that follow to assist you. Don't rely on your memory
of what needs to be proofed. Your goal is to generate perfect communications as quickly and efficiently as possible. Using the checklists will guide
you through the proofing process and help ensure that you don't forget to
proofread important elements.

Level One: Clarity and Grammar
Aaron, a medical equipment sales person, explained that he uses E-mail
for most of his internal correspondence. "It's quick and easy. A typical

example would be my asking a technician for an update on a prototype. The E-mail might be one line long, to one person, about one subject. It's imperative, however, that I be understood clearly. The consequences of a mistake are serious. The definition of a nightmare to me is if I have an appointment to show the prototype to a group of doctors, and surprise, I don't have the prototype in hand. Not only is it a waste of time, it's amateurish. It makes our whole company look unprepared and unprofessional. I must get accurate updates.

"Using the assessment to evaluate that one-line E-mail, I was surprised at what I learned. My scores were as follows."

1. Your communication will be distributed only within your organization. __5__
2. Using the Formality Index, you've determined that your communication is very informal. __3__
3. Your message is upbeat and fun. __3__
4. If your readers misunderstand your message, no negative consequences will result. __1__
5. Your communication is short. __5__
6. Your communication is simple. __5__
7. Your communication includes only one section. For example, it's a 100-word newsletter article, a business letter, a memo, or an E-mail with no attachments. __5__
8. Only one subject is included in your communication. __5__
9. Using the Matrix of Persuasion, you've determined that your readers are on your side and that they have the resources to do as you ask; in other words, you've assessed your writing task as Easy. __5__

"My total score was thirty-seven—Level One: Clarity and Grammar. Learning that was a big relief. I had been thinking that I needed to dissect every word of every sentence of every E-mail. Now I know that I don't. Even though the E-mail is crucial to my organization's success, as well as my own, I don't have to go crazy with proofreading. I just have to make sure my question is straightforward and unambiguous, and that my grammar is correct.

"Realizing that I should be proofing only to Level One standards made me focus more on writing simply and clearly in the first place. I'm careful to avoid euphemisms and long words. In other words, my writing got better by my learning the correct level of proofing."

Level One proofing usually includes the following:

1. Can your readers easily understand what you're asking them to do?
2. If 100 percent of your readers aren't familiar with your technical terms and industry jargon, have you defined them?
3. If 100 percent of your readers aren't familiar with your acronyms, have you explained them?
4. Have you confirmed that all numbers included in your communication are correct?
5. Have you avoided long or complicated sentences and sentence fragments (explained in Chapter Five)?
6. Are you certain that you've maintained noun/pronoun and subject/verb agreement (explained in Chapter Seven)?
7. Is your punctuation correct?
8. Are words capitalized properly?
9. Have you used your spell checker?
10. Have you reread your communication to catch missing words or phrases?

Level Two: Clarity, Grammar, Organization, and Completeness

Andrea, owner of a small insurance consulting firm, says, "My industry is pretty conservative, and I'm pretty traditional myself, so I use E-mail sparingly. Mostly, I write letters and send out proposals on letterhead.

"My letters are on a variety of subjects, from a letter of agreement to a cover letter accompanying a proposal. My proposals tend to focus on one project at a time and run about five to ten pages. I decided to see if I was proofing my letters and proposals carefully enough—or if I was overdoing it.

"Using the assessment to evaluate a letter of agreement to a new client, I was pleased at what I found out. My scores were as follows."

1. Your communication will be distributed only within your organization. __1__

2. Using the Formality Index, you've determined that your communication is very informal. __2__
3. Your message is upbeat and fun. __2__
4. If your readers misunderstand your message, no negative consequences will result. __2__
5. Your communication is short. __3__
6. Your communication is simple. __2__
7. Your communication includes only one section. For example,
   it's a 100-word newsletter article, a business letter, a memo, or
   an E-mail with no attachments. __5__
8. Only one subject is included in your communication. __5__
9. Using the Matrix of Persuasion, you've determined that your
   readers are on your side and that they have the resources to do
   as you ask; in other words, you've assessed your writing task as
   Easy. __3__

"My score totaled twenty-five—Level Two: Clarity, Grammar, Organization, and Completeness. Just what I thought. It was very reassuring
to know that I was on the right track—and I'm able to use the Level Two
checklist to help me proof the right things and not waste time proofing
things that don't matter. Letters of agreement need to be carefully worded
so as to leave no questions about the scope of work, delivery schedule,
prices, and responsibility.

"But having said that, it's pretty much a boilerplate letter. I change
the specifics, but most of it stays the same. I've used this format long
enough—for years—to know that it's a clear agreement and that the
grammar is correct.

"Proofing to confirm a solid organizational structure has proven valuable. Given that the letter is a boilerplate, I need to be certain that I don't
end up with a confusing mishmash every time I substitute paragraphs
and phrases.

"Proofing to Level Two standards takes a little time. But I've caught
errors that range from embarrassing, like including a past client's name,
to horrific, like agreeing to perform work that had nothing to do with the
actual project. It's completely worth the effort."

Level Two proofing includes all of Level One standards (see previous page), plus the following:

1. Did you select an appropriate organizational structure?
2. Does your message flow easily from paragraph to paragraph and from section to section?
3. Have you included any attachments, appendices, or corollary documents (such as a brochure) that you refer to in the body of your communication?
4. Have you considered the level of detail that's appropriate to include and are you providing it?
5. For those units of information that require detail, have you fully explained everything that needs to be described, outlined, or summarized?
6. Have you included all footnotes and endnotes that are referred to in the body of your communication?
7. If your document comprises multiple sections, are they consistently numbered and formatted?
8. If your document comprises multiple sections, are you including a table of contents, and is it correct?
9. Stop and think: Are you missing any pertinent units of information?
10. Reread your communication once again focusing on the overall message. Is it clear?

Level Three: Everything

Andrea, the owner of the insurance consulting firm who discovered that her boilerplate business letters needed to be proofed using Level Two standards says, "My proposals are more complex, even though I send out only one proposal per subject and they're not huge. Five to ten pages is quite modest by some proposal standards. I once saw a grant proposal that ran over a hundred pages. But still, this is my bread and butter. It is essential to me that my proposals are perfect in every way.

"I used the assessment to figure out what level of proofing is appropriate for my proposals—Level Two, like for my letters, or what. My scores were as follows."

1. Your communication will be distributed only within your organization. __1__

2. Using the Formality Index, you've determined that your communication is very informal. __2__
3. Your message is upbeat and fun. __1__
4. If your readers misunderstand your message, no negative consequences will result. __1__
5. Your communication is short. __1__
6. Your communication is simple. __1__
7. Your communication includes only one section. For example, it's a 100-word newsletter article, a business letter, a memo, or an E-mail with no attachments. __1__
8. Only one subject is included in your communication. __3__
9. Using the Matrix of Persuasion, you've determined that your readers are on your side and that they have the resources to do as you ask; in other words, you've assessed your writing task as Easy. __5__

"My score totaled sixteen—Level Three: Everything. This makes sense, given that my business success rides on my proposals convincing the 'powers that be' to hire my company. That means they have to be perfect in every way."

Proofing to Level Three standards includes assessing all of the elements listed in the checklists for Levels One and Two (see pages 128 and 130), plus the following:

1. Is your format correct?
2. Are there other items you could include, and if so, should you?
3. Consider how difficult or easy it is to read your text; is it an appropriate level of difficulty?
4. Are you using your readers' names enough? Are you using them too frequently?
5. Is your text specific enough to prove your points?
6. Have you evaluated the consistency of your sentences' grammatical constructions, bulleted lists, noun/pronoun agreement, subject/verb agreement, and other parallel construction issues?
7. Have you confirmed peoples' names by asking them if they're correct?
8. Have you added all information that could and should be included?

9. Are the margins correct, is the paper clean (or the E-mail intact), is the envelope of good quality, and are all aspects of the communication designed to achieve its objectives?

10. Have you looked at the document page by page to be certain that there are no awkward page breaks (for example, a section heading beginning at the bottom of a page)?

WHAT DO YOU KNOW? IT'S QUIZ TIME

Now that you know how to determine which level of editing is appropriate for your projects, it's time to discover whether you are able to identify common errors. The following quiz will help you assess your own level of knowledge about common grammar, punctuation, capitalization, and spelling issues.

It's important that you acknowledge your abilities—and inabilities—as a writer and proofreader. Until you know what errors you don't catch, and learn strategies to find problems and fix them, you won't be able to proofread effectively.

EXERCISE 19: *Assess Your Knowledge*
The following quiz is a test of your knowledge of grammar, word usage, punctuation, capitalization, and spelling, and of your proofreading abilities. Select the best answer for each of the questions. After the quiz, you'll find brief explanations of the correct answers. The next chapter goes into more detail and provides you with additional opportunities to practice.

1. The *disinterested/uninterested* student neglected to report that the vending machine *continually/continuously* ran out of juice.
   a. disinterested/continually
   b. disinterested/continuously
   c. uninterested/continually
   d. uninterested/continuously
2. The telecommunications manager investigated the complaint, he had questioned the explanation he'd heard.
   a. fragment—add conjunction

    b. comma splice—replace comma with a semicolon

    c. correct as is

3. Each of the supervisors _____ seven or more years of experience in the field.

    a. has

    b. have

4. Tammy knew _____ before she left the orchestra two years ago as a much-respected pianist whom most of the musicians adored.

    a. her

    b. she

5. Qualifying for the team last thursday meant she would leave school next winter and move to the west in order to compete.

    a. Qualifying for the team last Thursday meant she would leave school next winter and move to the west in order to compete.

    b. Qualifying for the team last Thursday meant she would leave school next Winter and move to the west in order to compete.

    c. Qualifying for the team last Thursday meant she would leave school next winter and move to the West in order to compete.

    d. Qualifying for the team last Thursday meant she would leave school next Winter and move to the West in order to compete.

6. Mae, a lawyer, wrote the E-mail and it was distributed to the officers.

    a. E-mail and, it

    b. E-mail, and it

    c. E-mail, and, it

    d. correct as is

7. The company had _____ busiest week of the year.

    a. it's

    b. its'

    c. its

8. Along with our colleagus, we will deciede about the warrenty and all pyament terms regarding the sail of business envelops.

    a. five words are misspelled

    b. six words are misspelled

    c. three words are misspelled

    d. four words are misspelled

9. Billy went dancing with Jo-Ann and _____.

    a. I

    b. myself

    c. me

10. Shouldn't this be labeled confidential?

    a. labeled "Confidential"?

    b. labeled "Confidential?"

    c. correct as is

Compare how you did with the correct answers below.

1. (c) The student's lack of concern is indicated by the word *neglected*. The vending machine emptied frequently and quickly, not nonstop.

2. (b) Given the options, this is the only answer. When two independent clauses are connected in this way, there are three punctuation alternatives:

   - Add a conjunction; in this example, the word *for*: The telecommunications manager investigated the complaint, for he had questioned the explanation he'd heard.
   - Use a semicolon: The telecommunications manager investigated the complaint; he had questioned the explanation he'd heard.
   - Separate into two sentences: The telecommunications manager investigated the complaint. He had questioned the explanation he'd heard.

3. (a) "Each" is the subject (the "doer") of the sentence, it is always singular, and it always takes a singular verb.

4. (a) Tammy is the subject (the "doer") of the sentence. "Knew" is the verb. The "musician" is the object of the sentence and thus takes the pronoun "her."

5. (c) Days of the week are always capitalized; seasons are capitalized only if used in a title (e.g., Summer Sale) or if personified (e.g., Old Man Winter). Regions of the country, like all geographic references, are capitalized.

6. (b) The comma goes before the coordinating conjunction when two independent clauses are connected.

7. (c) The word *it's* is a contraction of "it is." "Its" without an apostrophe is the possessive form of the word "it." "Its" is the only exception to the rule of how to punctuate possessives with apostrophes.

8. (b) There are six errors. The six errors are in italics: Along with our *colleagus* (should be *colleagues*), we will *deciede* (should be *decide*) about the *warrenty* (should be *warranty*) and all *pyament* (should be *payment*) terms regarding the *sail* (should be *sale*) of business *envelops* (should be *envelopes*). Note that your computer's spell checker would not have caught the misuse of *sail*; that's a usage error, not a spelling mistake.

9. (c) Prepositions (*with*) take the objective form of the pronoun (*me*).

10. (a) The word *confidential* should be capitalized. Question marks go outside the quotation marks unless what is within the quotation marks is a sentence. (In British English, punctuation always goes outside the quotation marks.)

How did you do? Whether you answered all ten questions correctly, or whether you made several errors, it's important that you understand that these are the most common errors made in business writing. Identify what you don't know and learn to do it correctly. Only by recognizing the limits of your knowledge can you identify what you need to learn. When your business writing is clear, correct, grammatical, and well organized, your professional image is enhanced. When your business writing is not clear, correct, grammatical, and well organized, your professional image suffers.

The next chapter updates your grammar and punctuation knowledge, alerting you to some recent changes. You'll learn some easy-to-remember tips to help you use the new rules, and you'll participate in several fun exercises to help you put the rules to work.

CHAPTER SEVEN

Proofread for Perfection

CONFIRM YOUR TEXT IS CLEAR AND PROFESSIONAL

In the last chapter, we reviewed different levels of proofreading. You learned how to determine which of the three levels of proofreading is appropriate for your various projects and how to check your work within each level. You also took a quiz to help you understand how much you know about common grammar and punctuation quandaries.

In this chapter, you'll learn strategies to remember the basic grammar, word usage, and capitalization rules for business writing. You'll also take part in several exercises to practice your proofreading and revision skills and to demonstrate that you can remember and use the rules.

English evolves quickly. Words come in and out of favor, and so do grammar and punctuation rules. By staying current with contemporary standards of business writing, you'll create a professional and polished image and avoid making embarrassing mistakes.

GRAMMAR AND PUNCTUATION UPDATE

Several grammar and punctuation rules have changed since you learned them in English class, and in order to produce professional writing, you need to be aware of the new criteria. The answers to the five questions that follow serve as guidelines to help you use up-to-date standards in your business writing.

The five questions are:

1. May I start a sentence with a transitional word such as *and* or *but*?
2. May I end a sentence with a preposition?

3. May I split an infinitive?
4. May I ever use *their* as a neutral pronoun?
5. How has comma usage changed since I left school?

Business Writing Should Be Conversational in Tone

In academic and the most formal writing, traditional standards—the formal ones we learned in school—still apply. In most kinds of business writing, however, the standard you should use to gauge excellence isn't adherence to academic or traditional rules—it's conversation: If you would speak it in a professional interaction, you can feel comfortable writing it. It's important to note that this standard, business conversation, does not imply that sloppy or incorrect grammar is acceptable. Just as you wouldn't speak with improper sentence structure or a lack of subject/verb agreement, for example, neither should you write that way.

Start Sentences with Words That Hook Your Readers' Interest

The first question is *May I start a sentence with a transitional word such as* and *and* or *but?* Many of us learned in school that we were never to begin sentences with words such as *and, but, because, so, therefore,* or any other transitional expression.

But just as in normal business conversations we begin sentences with *and, but, because, so, therefore,* and other similar words and phrases, it is accepted practice to use these words and phrases to begin sentences in business writing if doing so sounds natural and serves to emphasize your point. And as you may have noticed (but most readers do not), this paragraph and this sentence begin with these words, yet they read comfortably.

Angie, an administrative assistant in an insurance company, said, "It's such a relief to know that I can write the same way that I speak. I used to revise my drafts to a stodgy standard that sounded stilted and uninviting. Now I know I can maintain a conversational tone. And writing is quicker because I don't have to rewrite to add artificial formality.

"For example, instead of 'The Thanksgiving holiday requires that we extend the deadline for budget revisions. Please submit your revisions by December 1, 200x,' I'm able to write 'Because of Thanksgiving, the deadline for budget revisions has been extended to December 1.' Much better."

Let Sentences End Naturally

The second question is *May I end a sentence with a preposition?* In academic writing, you would never end a sentence with a preposition, but in conversation and in business writing, it is considered acceptable.

When asked if he considered it all right to end a sentence with a preposition, Sir Winston Churchill is credited with saying, "There are certain things up with which I will not put." His point, of course, is that it's absurd to *not* say, "There are certain things I will not put up with." Allowing the sentence to end with a preposition is often the best decision because it is the structure that sounds most natural. And as discussed above, if you would speak it in a professional interaction, you can feel comfortable writing it.

In making the decision to end your sentence with a preposition, read your sentence aloud while considering what points you intend to emphasize. In the example that follows, the writer needs to decide whether to create a formal or an informal tone. Both sentences are acceptable.

Option One (conversational, informal)
I'm trying to discover which station Paula's interview appeared on.

Option Two (conversational, formal)
I'm trying to discover on which station Paula's interview appeared.

Which do you prefer? The less formal or the more formal alternative? If you decide to avoid ending a sentence with a preposition, be certain that you don't create an awkward or stilted tone.

Karl, a landscape architect, explains, "I realized that many short statements and questions are best written with a preposition at the end. I used to drive myself crazy trying to avoid ending sentences with prepositions. Now, it's much easier to write. For instance, on my website, I have a section for frequently asked questions.

"Instead of 'Of what is compost made?' I wrote 'What is compost made of?' for instance. Another section of the website explains and recommends gardening tools. At first, I was concerned about titling it 'Tools You'll Want to Work With,' but it sounded right, so I went with it."

For further information about tricky situations involving prepositions, see Appendix B.

Try to Avoid Splitting Infinitives

Inserting an adverb between *to* and the verb, called *splitting the infinitive*, often results in awkward or confusing sentences. It frequently weakens your writing, although there are certain circumstances, discussed below, where it's an appropriate alternative.

For example, consider the sentence *He must strive* to even meet *the extended deadline*. The sentence is not only awkward in construction, it's unclear as well. Is he having trouble meeting the deadline or is the deadline unrealistic? Isn't it stronger and clearer to write *He must strive* to meet even *the extended deadline*?

Instead of *She always tries* to cautiously examine *antiques*, it's better to write *She always tries* to examine *antiques* cautiously.

Follow these steps to determine whether to split an infinitive:

1. Try putting the adverb after the infinitive. This approach is almost always the most effective strategy. In the two examples above, notice that putting the adverb after the infinitive improves the sentences.

2. If putting the adverb after the infinitive doesn't work, try putting it just before the infinitive.

Consider this sentence, for example: *I want you* to personally review *the project due to be completed in March*. To avoid splitting the infinitive, try moving the adverb *personally* after the infinitive. Here are two alternatives: *I want you* to review *the project due to be completed in March* personally. Or, *I want you* to review personally *the project due to be completed in March*. Both sentences are grammatical but awkward and unclear. Putting the adverb *personally* after the infinitive doesn't help.

Now try putting the adverb before the infinitive. In this example, the sentence would read: *I want you* personally to review *the project due to be completed in March*.

Positioning the adverb as indicated above, just before the infinitive, ensures that the meaning is clear and the sentence is constructed grammatically.

3. If putting the adverb before the infinitive still doesn't work, you may split the infinitive.

Consider this example: *You ought* to evaluate *the university's report to manage our technology needs* methodically. Or, *You ought* to evaluate methodically *the university's report to manage our technology needs*. Note that both examples read awkwardly.

Positioning the adverb in front of the infinitive results in another awkward sentence: *You ought* methodically to evaluate *the university's report to manage our technology needs*.

But note that splitting the infinitive works well: *You ought* to methodically evaluate *the university's report to manage our technology needs*.

Notice that the sentence reads naturally and your meaning is clear.

The three questions we've addressed thus far—starting sentences informally, ending sentences with prepositions, and splitting infinitives—are examples of business writing's drift toward informality and a conversational style. Using the professionally spoken word as your standard, you will create conversational text that's both accessible and appropriate.

POLITICALLY CORRECT WRITING

It's easy to become distracted from your purpose in writing by worrying that you'll offend various people or groups. The good news is that maintaining an appropriate tone is easier now than it used to be since gender-neutral terms such as firefighter (instead of fireman) and letter carrier (instead of postman) have become common in our language. But we still lack a neutral pronoun, so you need to decide how you'll handle references to men and women in your writing.

Rewrite Sentences to Avoid Misusing *Their*

The fourth question is *May I ever use* their *as a neutral pronoun?* The answer is no. Even though many people use the word their as a gender-neutral pronoun in business conversation, employing this usage in writing should be avoided; it is considered too informal. There's no question that English lacks a gender-neutral pronoun and that it would be handy to have one. The question is what to do without it. Consider, for example, this sentence:

Mohammed and Hannah have initiated a discussion project so that each Arab and Jew is able to discuss his feelings about the Mideast crisis.

Do you see the problem? Not all Arabs and Jews are men. The pronoun "his" is intended to represent all people, and using it in this way is grammatically correct. But it's politically incorrect, and it may be confusing. Some people, after reading that sentence, may think that Mohammed and Hannah are arranging for a group of men to discuss the Mideast crisis.

A better solution is to rewrite the sentence to reflect a plural rather than a singular reference, as shown here:

Mohammed and Hannah have initiated a discussion project so that all Arabs and Jews are able to discuss their feelings about the Mideast crisis.

What do you think about this revision? Isn't it better?

Revising from a singular to a plural reference to avoid confusing or inaccurate implications is always a good idea, and sometimes it's crucial. Note that in the following example, the lack of a neutral singular pronoun results in an odd structure:

Morris, a pianist, and Sophie, a flutist, each won a scholarship for his musical ability.

Obviously the sentence must be rewritten. How about this?

Morris, a pianist, and Sophie, a flutist, both won scholarships for their musical abilities.

Sometimes rewriting the sentence is tougher. For example:

The featured speaker will address the chemical disposal problem and how their company is handling it.

If you don't know who the featured speaker will be, what do you do? Do you use "his or her," highlighting that the speaker hasn't yet been selected? Or do you allow the use of the word *their*? One possibility is to rewrite the sentence:

The featured speaker will address the chemical disposal problem and how to handle it.

Better? Most people agree that avoiding the issue is the better alternative in business writing, and the easiest way to avoid the issue is to make sure that you use "he" only when the reference refers to a singular male.

PUNCTUATE FOR CLARITY

Punctuate to ensure that your meaning is clear. Inserting punctuation marks consistently helps your reader understand your intent. There are several rules, but many punctuation issues are a matter of opinion or style: There is more than one acceptable alternative. By deciding how you'll handle these style dilemmas once and for all, you'll save time and ensure clarity. Once you know which rules you need to follow, you are in a good position to make decisions that suit you and to apply them consistently.

In this section, we'll discuss the fifth question, *How has comma usage changed since I left school?*, as well as clarify other punctuation issues that frequently arise in business writing.

Use Commas to Separate Units of Information

Commas indicate a pause in the sentence. In business writing, you need to use commas in the following circumstances:

1. to separate independent clauses
2. to separate dependent and independent clauses
3. to separate a quote from its attribution
4. to set aside intervening, modifying phrases
5. to separate units within a list (sometimes a semicolon is required)

These five circumstances account for most of the comma usage in business writing. By learning these rules and adhering to them, your writing will be polished and professional.

You Have Three Choices in Punctuating Compound Sentences

Whenever two or more independent clauses (i.e., phrases that could stand alone as sentences) are joined together, there are always three punctuation options.

1. Split them into separate sentences.
2. Use a semicolon to separate the clauses.
3. Use a comma before the conjunction that connects the clauses.

Consider, for example, the following sentence. Notice how it can be punctuated—properly—three ways. There is no right or best choice among the three; they're all acceptable alternatives. As you read them, ask yourself which one you like best and why.

1. Mindy wanted to apply for the newly created position. Tom did not.
2. Mindy wanted to apply for the newly created position; Tom did not.
3. Mindy wanted to apply for the newly created position, but Tom did not.

The first option, separating the two clauses, results in a short second sentence that serves to emphasize Tom's stance. The second option employs a semicolon to show that the sentences are intimately connected. The third option adds a conjunction to show the relationship between the two sentences.

Choose the one that seems best to you and that most reflects your meaning.

Separate a Dependent Clause from an Independent Clause

A dependent clause at the beginning of a sentence should be separated from the independent clause that follows it by a comma. (Dependent clauses often start with the words *after, although, as, because, if, since, when,* or *while,* among other words.)

- Although Mr. Samuels meant it for the best, his comment was counterproductive.
- As it turned out, we were able to attend the conference.
- Because of the change in leadership, the project deadline was extended.

If a dependent clause follows or interrupts an independent clause, the clauses are not separated by commas if the dependent clause is essential to the meaning of the sentence (a restrictive clause). If the dependent clause is not essential to the meaning (nonrestrictive), commas should by used to separate it from the independent clause.

- The Farrow Corporation proposal arrived after we had selected our new supplier. (The dependent clause "after we had selected our new supplier" provides essential information about when the proposal arrived; therefore, no comma precedes it.)
- We can discuss our next step in person or, if you'd prefer, via E-mail. (The dependent clause "if you'd prefer" is separated from the independent clause by commas because it is nonrestrictive.)

Use Commas to Indicate a Quote

Quotation marks should only be used for a speaker's exact words. Don't modify words if you're going to use quotation marks. The following example shows the correct use of commas when quoting a speaker.

In her opening remarks, Ms. Kingsley said, "As I said a year ago, business is great!"

Notice the positions of the three commas in the sentence:

1. after the introductory prepositional phrase (*In her opening remarks*)
2. between the attribution of the quote and the quote (*Ms. Kingsley said*)
3. after the opening dependent clause within the quote (*As I said a year ago*)

Once you understand where commas need to go and why, putting them there is fairly straightforward.

Separate Modifying Phrases

Modifying phrases add information, often providing valuable or interesting details that clarify or expand ideas. Setting off these phrases with punctuation helps the reader understand the relationship between the modification and the main thought.

Whenever you punctuate a modifying phrase, there are always three options, and the marks are properly used in pairs.

1. Use commas to convey neutrality.
2. Use parentheses to indicate that the modifying phrase is an aside.
3. Use dashes to highlight an abrupt change or to add emphasis.

Consider how the meaning of the sentence below changes when it's punctuated these three different ways:

1. Tyra, recipient of last year's Employee of the Year award, made the arrangements for the annual banquet.
2. Tyra (recipient of last year's Employee of the Year award) made the arrangements for the annual banquet.
3. Tyra—recipient of last year's Employee of the Year award—made the arrangements for the annual banquet.

The information that Tyra won the award is delivered in three distinct ways. In the first example, the information about the award is presented in a matter-of-fact manner, as indicated by the commas. In the second example, the information is presented as an aside; it's downplayed, as indicated by the parentheses. Dashes, used in the third example, suggest that the information is hot news, as if it's being hollered from the rooftops.

Make your choice based on the meaning you intend to convey: commas are neutral, parentheses whisper, and dashes yell.

Commas Help Separate Units Within a List

When three or more items are listed, use commas to separate them. For example, note the punctuation of the following sentence:

During the relocation, Alice will supervise the packing, trucking, and unpacking efforts.

It is considered optional to use the serial comma (before the word *and*), but it is recommended because serial commas clarify meaning—in this case, that the unpacking activities are separate from the packing and trucking activities. If you decide to use the comma in this way, be certain to do so consistently throughout your document.

It's best to use semicolons to separate units when there are commas within the units. In the following example, notice that the sentence's meaning is clearer when it is punctuated with semicolons.

> It was decided that team leaders would include Amanda, East Coast, Sam, West Coast, Gloria, Mid Atlantic, and Cal, South.

> It was decided that team leaders would include Amanda, East Coast; Sam, West Coast; Gloria, Mid Atlantic; and Cal, South.

EXERCISE 20: *Revise for Clarity*

Revise the following sentences to make the copy less stilted, avoid split infinitives, and ensure proper punctuation.

1. Mr. Wexler always tries to fully investigate the causes of a company's bankruptcy.
2. Julia without her Tom is nothing.
3. Kyu-Ja said Linda What time is the train expected to arrive?
4. It has come to our attention that Marybeth from Dallas Charlie from Portland Dee from Chicago and Brian from Phoenix all need to meet with the advertising team.
5. Each of the supervisors is qualified to lead his team.

How did you do? There are some tricky issues in these five sentences. Without knowing the writer's intention, you'll have a tough time revising copy. Remember to start your revision with a clear understanding of the writer's meaning.

1. Mr. Wexler always tries to fully investigate the causes of a company's bankruptcy.

The split infinitive is awkward. It is better to write the sentence as:

Mr. Wexler always tries to investigate fully the causes of a company's bankruptcy.

2. Julia without her Tom is nothing.

There are several ways to punctuate this sentence, depending on the writer's intention. For example, you could write:

Julia: Without her, Tom is nothing.
Julia, without her Tom, is nothing.

In other words, who's dependent on the other person for substance? Is Tom nothing without Julia or is Julia nothing without Tom?

3. Kyu-Ja said Linda What time is the train expected to arrive?

You need to know who's speaking in order to properly punctuate this sentence. Here are two alternatives:

"Kyu-Ja," said Linda. "What time is the train expected to arrive?"
Kyu-Ja said, "Linda! What time is the train expected to arrive?"

4. It has come to our attention that Marybeth from Dallas Charlie from Portland Dee from Chicago and Brian from Phoenix all need to meet with the advertising team.

Add commas as follows:

It has come to our attention that Marybeth from Dallas, Charlie from Portland, Dee from Chicago, and Brian from Phoenix all need to meet with the advertising team.

5. Each of the supervisors is qualified to lead his team.

You'll probably want to revise this to make it gender-neutral. If all the supervisors are men, this is fine as written, but most likely all the supervisors are not men, and therefore the issue must be addressed.

All the supervisors are qualified to lead their teams.

USING PROPER GRAMMAR
SIGNALS PROFESSIONALISM

When your grammar is sloppy, your readers will think either that you don't know what's correct or that you don't care. When you follow the standard rules, you will be perceived as professional, and your readers will have more confidence in you and your ideas. Two of the most common grammar errors involve subject/verb agreement and noun/pronoun agreement.

Subjects and Verbs Must Agree

Subjects and verbs must agree in person and in number all the time—there are no exceptions. The subject of the sentence, that is, the doer of the action, must match the verb. A singular subject requires a singular verb; a plural subject requires a plural verb.

The rule is straightforward, but applying it can be tricky. Where people get into the most trouble is with intervening modifying phrases, certain specific words (such as *each* and *every*), and collective nouns.

Ignore Phrases and Clauses That Separate Subjects from Verbs
Intervening, modifying phrases often add interesting details or important qualifications. However, it's easy to become confused about which word in a sentence is the subject. For example, consider this sentence:

> The briefcase (subject, singular) containing all the reports was (verb, singular) in Max's car.

It's easy to see why you might be confused; the noun closest to the verb is plural ("reports"). Nevertheless, the modifying phrase "containing all the reports" should be ignored in making the subject/verb agreement decision. Note that without that phrase, the sentence reads:

> The briefcase (subject, singular) was (verb, singular) in Max's car.

Subject/verb agreement doesn't change when you add intervening, modifying phrases, so it makes sense to eliminate them when making the determination.

Supervisors (subject, plural), especially those who are new to the field, have (verb, plural) to attend orientation.

When you eliminate the intervening phrase, you're left with:

Supervisors (subject, plural) have (verb, plural) to attend orientation.

Follow the Rules No Matter How It Sounds to Your Ear

Many people make subject/verb agreement errors because they mistakenly trust their ear. But your ear may have been trained to hear something as correct when it's not. Be certain that your ear guides you correctly before relying on "how it sounds." Mistakes frequently occur when using specific words that are always, by definition, either singular or plural.

For example, use a singular verb after *each, everyone, everybody, nobody, someone, every, one, another,* and *much.* Use a plural verb after *few, many, others,* and *several.*

Every supervisor is attending. (singular)
Everybody enjoys orientation. (singular)
Several supervisors are out of the office. (plural)
Many were interviewed, but few were able to answer. (plural)

Collective Nouns May Take a Singular or Plural Verb

A collective noun refers to a group. If the group is acting as one unit, the noun is treated as singular. If the group's members are acting individually, the noun is treated as plural. (In British English, collective nouns are treated as plurals.)

The Technical Review Board meets in May. (The subject is "Board," one unit, singular.)

The company is one of the largest employers in California. (The subject is "company," one unit, singular.)

My family are doing well. (The subject is "family," the individuals are emphasized, plural.)

Collective nouns include *committee, company, board, firm, jury, crowd, staff, group, family, audience, public,* and *team,* among many others.

Nouns and Pronouns Must Agree

A noun and a pronoun must agree in number and in person, regardless of where in the sentence the words occur. Most people can trust their ear to understand the basics. Where most difficulties occur are in the proper usage of *who* and *whom,* in the lack of a gender-neutral pronoun (discussed earlier), and with collective nouns.

Use Who *and* Whom *Properly*

The use of *who* and *whom* has, surprisingly, not evolved out of written usage. Most people are uncomfortable making the *who/whom* determination and know they can't trust their ear to guide them.

In fact, the rules are clear and relatively easy to understand and remember. The basic rule is that you should use *who* or *whoever* when the word you're replacing is the subject of the sentence or the subject of a dependent clause (when you can substitute *he, she, they, I,* or *we*). Use *whom* or *whomever* when the word you're replacing is the object of a verb or a preposition (when you can substitute *him, her, them, me,* or *us*).

Consider these examples:

Who was there?
I will respond to *whoever* provides the answers.
You saw *whom*?
I will consult with *whomever* I want.

The easiest way to confirm that you're using *who* and *whom* correctly is to follow this three-step process:

1. Identify all the verbs in the sentence.
2. Identify all the subjects that go with these verbs.
3. If the word you're looking to replace is the subject of the sentence or a dependent clause, use *who* or *whoever*. If the word you're looking to replace is not the subject, use *whom* or *whomever*.

There is only one exception: The verb *to be* requires the use of *who* regardless of where it appears in the sentence. For example, in analyzing whether to replace *him* (or *her*) with *who* or *whom* in the following sentence, use the three-step model:

I know him. (or "her")

1. The verb is "know."
2. The subject is "I."
3. The word *him* (or *her*) is not the subject of the sentence; therefore, it is correct to use *whom*.

I know whom?

But now consider replacing the word *he* (or *she*) with *who* or *whom* in this sentence:

I am he. (or "she")

1. The verb is "am."
2. The subject is "I."
3. The word *he* (or *she*) is not the subject of the sentence; therefore, it would seem to be correct to use *whom*. However, the word *am* is a form of the verb *to be* and as such is the exception to the rule. Thus it is correct to write:

I am who?

Use this three-step process to analyze sentences until you have trained your ear sufficiently to make the determination automatically. If you're alert for the one exception (any form of the verb *to be*), you should find it easy to make the *who/whom* determination correctly every time.

Collective Nouns Are Singular When Acting as One Unit

Remember to watch for collective nouns (discussed earlier), words referring to groups of people or things. Notice that in every example that follows, the pronoun is singular.

The *jury* rendered *its* verdict on Tuesday.
The *company* changed *its* policy.
The *firm* relocated *its* distribution center.

Collective nouns are treated as singular when the group represented by the collective noun acts as one unit.

EXERCISE 21: *Correct Common Grammar Errors*
Complete the following sentences, ensuring proper subject/verb and noun/pronoun agreement.

1. Roberta said she'd go to work for _____ paid her the most money.
   (whoever/whomever)
2. The cabinet, along with the files, _____ to Willy.
   (belong/belongs)
3. The staff expressed _____ support for the merger.
   (its/their)
4. You went to the party with _____?
   (who/whom)
5. The mayor, as well as his deputies, _____ the initiative was a success.
   (say/says)
6. Neither the conductor nor the pianist _____aware of the schedule change.
   (is/are)
7. _____ should I consult?
   (Who/Whom)
8. The report, with all of its attachments, _____ a strong case for our position.
   (create/creates)
9. I'll go to the meeting with _____ leaves first.
   (whoever/whomever)
10. None of us _____ driving to Texas.
    (is/are)

How did you do? Here are the correct answers:

1. Roberta said she'd go to work for __whoever__ paid her the most money.

The verb "paid" needs a subject to go with it, thus you need to use *whoever*. Don't be distracted by the preposition "for." Follow the three-step method discussed above.

2. The cabinet, along with the files, __belongs__ to Willy.

Eliminate the modifying phrase "along with the files" to ensure you correctly identify the subject as "cabinet."

3. The staff expressed __its__ support for the merger.

"Staff" is a collective noun and is treated here as singular.

4. You went to the party with __whom__?

The only verb, "went," goes with the subject "you." Therefore, *whom* is correct, as it serves as the object of the preposition "with."

5. The mayor, as well as his deputies, __says__ the initiative was a success.

The subject of the sentence is "mayor," a singular noun. Eliminate the phrase "as well as his deputies" to confirm that the correct choice is *says*.

6. Neither the conductor nor the pianist __is__ aware of the schedule change.

"Neither" is singular if both subjects are singular.

7. __Whom__ should I consult?

The verb is "should consult." The subject is "I." Given there is no other verb, and the verb is not a form of *to be*, the pronoun *whom* is correct.

8. The report, with all of its attachments, ___creates___ a strong case for our position.

Eliminate the modifying phrase "with all of its attachments" and you'll discover that the subject of the sentence is "report," a singular noun.

9. I'll go to the meeting with ___whoever___ leaves first.

The verb "leaves" lacks a subject; therefore, you need to use *whoever*. That *whoever* also serves as the object of the preposition "with" is secondary; its primary job is to serve as the subject of "leaves." When one word serves two purposes—an object of a preposition and a subject of a verb, as in this sentence—the subject is considered more important; thus it is proper to use *whoever*.

10. None of us ___is___ driving to Texas.

"None" is always singular in formal writing.

USE THE CORRECT WORD

There are many words that are easily confused with one another and frequently misused. Learning which word to use in which circumstance ensures you don't make embarrassing mistakes. Read the explanations of correct usage below and focus on the tricks to remember which word to use when.

affect/effect
Probably the most misused words in business communications are *affect* and *effect*. The confusion occurs because both words can be used as nouns or verbs. Most often you will use *affect* as a verb and *effect* as a noun.

Note that the *a* in *affect* is like the *a* in *action*, and that's what *affect* the verb represents—an action word. Here's an example of *affect* used as a verb:

The speed of downloading an attachment is *affected* by available bandwidth.

The *e* in *effect* is like the *e* in *end* result, and that's what *effect* the noun represents—an outcome, or end result. The following sentence shows *effect* used as a noun:

One **effect** of the clever advertising campaign was that sales went up.

Occasionally, you will see *effect* used as a verb (meaning to bring about) in business writing. For instance, *How will Mr. Morrison effect change within his organization?* illustrates *effect* being used as a verb. Likewise, occasionally you will see *affect* used as a noun (meaning a feeling or emotion as distinguished from cognition). A director might say that an actress lacks *affect*, for example.

It's important to recognize these different applications; however, for most of us in most business writing situations, using *affect* as a verb (action) and *effect* as a noun (end result) simplifies the process and satisfies our needs.

- *Affect* (v) means to influence, to change.
- *Effect* (n) refers to results.

A country's commitment to protect its rain forests **affects** (verb) whether ecotourism is viable.
A common **effect** (noun) of a country's commitment to protect its rain forests is the need to identify new sources of revenue.

among/between

Note the *tw* in the word *between*. The *tw* in *between* is like the *tw* in the word *two*. The reference to the number *two* makes it easy to remember when to use *between* and when to use *among*.

- *Among* is used for more than two.
- *Between* is used in connection with two persons or things.

He divided the assignment *among* the three managers.
He divided the assignment *between* the two managers.

continual/continuous

Think of the sound gently running water makes. That soft *s-s-s-s* sound is similar to the *s-s-s-s* sound in the word *continuous*. And just as a little stream is always flowing, the word *continuous* means "always in action." *Continual*, by contrast, indicates stops and starts.

- *Continual* refers to an action that occurs with pauses.
- *Continuous* refers to an action that occurs without pauses.

The archaic phone system *continually* breaks down.
The new security system operates *continuously*.

eager/anxious

Eager is a positive word; *anxious* is a negative word. The way you can remember which is which is that the *e* in *eager* is like the *e* in *enthusiastic*, and that's what *eager* means. The *a* in *anxious* is like the *a* in *apprehensive*, and that's that *anxious* means. Part of the confusion stems from the fact that sometimes you feel both *eager* and *anxious* at the same time. For instance, if long-lost relatives are coming for a weekend visit, you probably feel *eager* to see them. But it wouldn't be a surprise if you also feel *anxious*.

- *Eager* means enthusiastic.
- *Anxious* means apprehensive, worried, or filled with anxiety.

Erin was *eager* for the party to begin.
Her coworkers were *anxious* about her health.

farther/further

Think of the physical distance associated with the word *far*. That's what *farther* means: physical distance. *Further* refers to *extent* and should be used with nonphysical measures.

- *Farther* refers to physical distance.
- *Further* refers to degree or extent. (You might think of it as mental distance.)

Katie can run *farther* than most people on her team.
Ali pursues a philosophical discussion *further* than most people.

lay/lie

The word *lay* needs to be followed by a direct object, whereas the word *lie* is followed by an indication of direction. Remember this difference by keeping in mind that *lie* and *direction* both have the letter *i* as their second letter.

- *Lay* means to put or place something somewhere.
- *Lie* means to rest or recline.

Please *lay* your report on the stack to the left.
We asked the sick employee to *lie* down.

less/fewer

Fewer, used with plural nouns, refers to number. *Less*, used with singular nouns, refers to degree or amount. Both *fewer* and *number* end in *er*, which can help you remember which word to use. Part of the confusion results from the commonly seen sign in grocery stores: "ten items or less." It should read: "ten items or fewer."

- *Less* is used for quantities and degree.
- *Fewer* is used for numbers (countable units).

There were *fewer* applicants for the job.
There was *less* completion.
You must make *fewer* mistakes in order to keep your job.
I trust there will be *less* cause for complaint.

EXERCISE 22: *Practice Using Frequently Misused Words*

Read the sentences that follow and choose the appropriate word. Try to complete the exercise without rereading the word usage explanations to see whether you remember the rules.

1. The fax machine (continually/continuously) runs out of paper.
2. Bring (less/fewer) muffins for next week's staff meeting.
3. How will the decision to streamline operations (affect/effect) the workforce?
4. Just (among/between) the three of us, what do you think about the proposal?

5. We are (eager/anxious) to receive our tax refund.
6. He ran (farther/further) than anyone else in the company race.
7. When you finish reading the newsletter, please (lay/lie) it on my desk.

How did you do? Were you able to correctly identify the proper word choices?

1. The fax machine *continually* runs out of paper.
   Sometimes the fax machine has plenty of paper.
2. Bring *fewer* muffins for next week's staff meeting.
   The word *muffins* is plural, so *fewer* is the appropriate choice.
3. How will the decision to streamline operations *affect* the workforce?
   As a verb, *affect* signals action and is the proper word.
4. Just *among* the three of us, what do you think about the proposal?
   Between would be used if there were only two people.
5. We are *eager* to receive our tax refund.
   Depending on the circumstances, you might feel anxious about receiving a tax refund. For example, if you have many bills and are planning to use your refund to pay off some debts, while waiting for it to arrive you may feel anxious. However, one would expect you to feel more excitement than anxiety about receiving money, so *eager* is probably the better word choice. It's important to note, however, that the choice should be made based on the writer's intent, not speculation.
6. He ran *farther* than anyone else in the company race.
   Farther relates to physical distance.
7. When you finish reading the newsletter, please *lay* it on my desk.
   The word *lay* is followed by the object "it," referring to the newsletter.

CAPITALIZE FOR EMPHASIS

If you capitalize all letters within an E-mail, you're likely to hear from your reader, "Stop shouting at me!" All caps are considered "shouting."

When you capitalize a word you are adding emphasis or importance, or otherwise highlighting the word. Be cautious about conveying the significance resulting from capitalizing a word. The points that follow outline when it's proper to capitalize words and when it's considered optional. (Note that you don't capitalize seasons [except in a title or if personified] or directionals. Compass points, when abbreviated, are capitalized.)

Here are ten common capitalization issues you're likely to run into in business writing.

1. Capitalize official titles of honor and respect when they precede personal names.

   Princess Diana vs. Diana, the princess
   Ms. Mary Watkins
   President Washington vs. Washington, the first president of the United States of America

2. Capitalizing job titles is generally not recommended by style guides, although many companies do so. If you do, be consistent. If a job title precedes the job holder's name, then capitalize it.

   Chairman Frank Donahue vs. Frank Donahue, chairman of the committee

3. Capitalize the first, last, and all important words in a title. (Use italics to indicate a book, play, or movie title; place article titles within quotation marks.)

   Jane K. Cleland is the author of *Business Writing for Results*.
   Have you seen *A Funny Thing Happened on the Way to the Forum* on Broadway?

4. Capitalize the name of all governmental agencies whether using the complete name or a shortened version of the name.

   We can get the licensing requirements from the Department of Motor Vehicles.

After completing your tax forms, send them to the Internal
Revenue Service.

5. Capitalize all academic degrees following a name (whether
abbreviated or written out) and all academic and religious titles.

William Andres, Ph.D.
Bishop Daniel Smyth
Alice Jones-Peterson, Certified Financial Planner
Professor Al Walker
Mohammed Aveki, M.D.
Billy Peterson, CPA

6. Capitalize all trade names. You'll need to go to the source for
this, and you should capitalize all words exactly as the organization does.

Cardmembers may qualify for our prestigious and exclusive
program, the Preferred Members Club.
We own a Xerox copier.
Do you like Post-it Notes?

7. Capitalize all official building names, streets, planets, heavenly
bodies, continents, regions of a country, cities, states, countries,
landforms, bodies of water, and any public place.

Many companies have their headquarters in the Empire State
Building in New York City.
Have you visited Central Park?
A trip down the Nile River would be invigorating; then we could
proceed to Lake Victoria in our tour of Africa. Or would you prefer
to go to the Far East?
Mars is currently being studied; someday we'll understand the
entire Milky Way.
I took Route 95 all the way to Maine.
The World Wide Web makes researching health issues easier. (Note:
the Web is considered a place, and thus it's proper to capitalize it.)

8. Capitalize names, nicknames, and family appellations.

> The reunion will be organized by Aunt Agnes. Brent; my Little Cookie, Emily; Nana-Jasmine, Grandpa's new wife; and I will help with the cooking.

9. Capitalize the days of the week, months of the year, holidays, and holy days.

> I'm surprised at how late Easter is this year.
> It's fun to pick apples in October; Tuesday or Wednesday is best because there are fewer people.

10. Capitalize historical periods, events, epithets, and documents.

> It dates from the Regency.
> He fought in the Civil War.
> One of history's great warriors was Alexander the Great.
> The United States of America was founded when the Declaration of Independence was signed.

EXERCISE 23: *Capitalize Correctly*

Rewrite the sentences below, making all appropriate corrections.

1. the team leader is ms. feeney.
2. the keynote speaker, dr. leon williams, chairman, will speak on wednesday.
3. the first draft of the budget is due friday, january 1.
4. payments for unemployment taxes are sent to the new york department of taxation.
5. uncle joel and aunt maria are staying at the sheraton hotel on the avenue of the americas.
6. i just finished watching cnn news on channel 2.
7. we want to visit red rocks when we take our western road trip next spring.
8. please order scotch tape for the president.
9. his office is located on royal street, which is one block from bourbon street in the french quarter in new orleans.

10. please read the article "building your computer."

Compare your decisions with the following revised sentences. There were some tricky issues here that reflect the kinds of difficulties you're likely to run into when making capitalization decisions for business communications.

1. The team leader is Ms. Feeney.
2. The keynote speaker, Dr. Leon Williams, chairman, will speak on Wednesday.
3. The first draft of the budget is due Friday, January 1.
4. Payments for unemployment taxes are sent to the New York Department of Taxation.
5. Uncle Joel and Aunt Maria are staying at the Sheraton Hotel on the Avenue of the Americas.
6. I just finished watching CNN News on channel 2.
7. We want to visit Red Rocks when we take our western road trip next spring.
8. Please order Scotch tape for the president.
9. His office is located on Royal Street, which is one block from Bourbon Street in the French Quarter in New Orleans.
10. Please read the article "Building Your Computer."

In this chapter, we've covered the essential rules that govern and the decisions that need to be made in business writing. You've learned key punctuation, grammar, word usage, and capitalization standards, along with tips on how to remember the rules. Take the following quiz to discover how much you've learned and remember about creating professional communications.

EXERCISE 24: *What Did You Learn?*

Choose the best answer for each of the following questions.

1. Did you add the title, implications of computerizing customer service, to the article manuscript?
   a. title, "implications of computerizing customer service"
   b. title, "Implications of Computerizing Customer Service"

c. title, "Implications Of Computerizing Customer Service"

d. correct as is

2. Every one of the associates _____ training to keep current with technology.

   a. need

   b. needs

3. Head north because the winter special is only available in the northeast starting in january.

   a. Head north because the winter special is only available in the northeast starting in January.

   b. Head North because the Winter special is only available in the Northeast starting in January.

   c. Head north because the winter special is only available in the Northeast starting in January.

   d. correct as is

4. The administrator knew it was a problem, he told his boss right away.

   a. add a conjunction

   b. replace the comma with a semicolon

   c. correct as is

   d. a or b

5. The supervisor thought about it and she determined the expense was justified.

   a. about it and, she

   b. about it, and she

   c. about it, and,

   d. correct as is

6. Marion Silver, _____ most of the other employees admire as a hard worker, left early.

   a. whom

   b. who

7. Dr. Ortiz, author of more than thirty books, _____ to join the faculty.

   a. want

   b. wants

8. Helena, Montana, San Francisco, California, Rome, New York, and Paris, Texas, are all cities in the United States.

   a. correct as is

b. replace commas after the states with semicolons

c. use dashes after the cities

d. either b or c

9. The company had _____ most profitable year ever.

    a. it's

    b. its

    c. their

10. The committee chair asked the members to meticulously review the proposal.

    a. correct as is

    b. to review meticulously

    c. meticulously to review

    d. to review the proposal meticulously

Were you able to answer the questions? Compare your answers to the following.

1. Did you add the title, "Implications of Computerizing Customer Service," to the article manuscript?

The correct answer is b. Because "of" is not a key word, it is not capitalized. The title is in quotation marks because it's an article title. (Set book titles in italics.)

2. Every one of the associates needs training to keep current with technology.

The correct answer is b. "Every" is singular and thus requires the singular form of the verb *need* to maintain subject/verb agreement.

3. Head north because the winter special is only available in the Northeast starting in January.

The correct answer is c. Northeast is capitalized because it's a geographic region, not a direction.

4. The administrator knew it was a problem, so he told his boss right away.

Or: The administrator knew it was a problem; he told his boss right away.

The correct answer is d. The sentence could be corrected with a conjunction, such as *so*, or a semicolon.

    5. The supervisor thought about it, and she determined the expense was justified.

The correct answer is b. When connecting two independent clauses with a conjunction, add a comma before the conjunction.

    6. Marion Silver, whom most of the other employees admire as a hard worker, left early.

The correct answer is a. The verb "left" goes with the subject "Marion Silver." "Whom" is the object of the verb "admire."

    7. Dr. Ortiz, author of more than thirty books, wants to join the faculty.

The correct answer is b. Eliminate the modifying phrase "author of more than thirty books," and the sentence reads "Dr. Ortiz wants to join the faculty."

    8. Helena, Montana; San Francisco, California; Rome, New York; and Paris, Texas, are all cities in the United States.

The correct answer is b. Replacing the commas after the states (except for the last one) with semicolons will help ensure clarity.

    9. The company had its most profitable year ever.

The correct answer is b. The collective noun "company" takes the singular possessive "its."

    10. The committee chair asked the members to review the proposal meticulously.

The correct answer is d. It is the only alternative where the meaning is clear and the construction isn't awkward.

In this chapter you've learned and practiced the basic grammar, punctuation, word usage, and capitalization rules you need to know in business writing. You've become familiar with common pitfalls and discovered tricks to remember the rules.

In our final chapter, we're going to pull together everything we've discussed thus far. You'll use the systems and strategies you've learned to write and revise a business communication.

CHAPTER EIGHT

Write with Confidence

PUTTING IT ALL TOGETHER:
USE THE THREE-STEP PROCESS

In the last chapter, we reviewed common grammar, punctuation, word usage, and capitalization errors and discussed strategies to remember the rules.

In this chapter, you'll put all the tools we've discussed to work. You'll practice writing a report, and you'll compare your approach to another writer's strategy. You'll see firsthand how using the three-step process as a framework allows you to work productively.

A METHODICAL APPROACH

The tools you've learned in this book serve as a framework for the writing process. To see how the tools function together, you're going to be asked to work alongside Brad, the vice president of risk management for a Florida-based firm. Brad's company manufactures customized novelty gift items and is looking to build a new factory. Brad needs to write a report to present as a handout to his company's executive committee.

While you might lack Brad's expertise in risk management, you can assume the information provided in this chapter is accurate and complete. Use the tools checklist below to guide you as you write.

Step One: Get Your Thoughts in Order

✓ Answer the question, "What do I want my readers to do as a result of reading this report?"

✓ Analyze your audience by considering their personalities and by using the Formality Index.

✓ Assess your writing assignment with the Matrix of Persuasion.

Step Two: Create a Draft on Paper (or on Your Computer)

✓ Organize your thoughts.

✓ Use the Hub & Spokes model to get your thoughts on paper. Once done, select your beginning and ending paragraphs.

✓ Generate a first draft.

Step Three: Revise for Clarity

✓ Revise to a second draft with the Empathy Index, and focus on the lead and salutation.

✓ Add a snappy close. (And consider adding a P.S., addendum, appendix, enclosures, or attachments.)

✓ Make the writing specific.

✓ Select the best words using the principle of FURY.

✓ Ensure the writing is concise, clear, positive, and parallel.

✓ Check your grammar, punctuation, word usage, and capitalization.

✓ Make the draft visually appealing.

✓ Read the entire draft.

Review the following summary of Brad's project. After you complete each step, compare your work to Brad's.

Brad's Point of View

Brad's job is to oversee the enterprise risk management process within his company. "All corporations have to manage risk," Brad explains. "In our company, with our complex exposures, it's much more complicated than simply calling an insurance agent. My job is to identify risks, quantify our exposure, and recommend risk reduction and risk management strategies.

"The project I'm working on now is looking at factory building site alternatives from a risk perspective. I've made my decision; now I need to write a report explaining why I think we should build our new factory in Georgia, not in Florida or Illinois. I'm scheduled to present my results and explain my recommendation to the executive committee. This decision is a very big deal. It will affect the course of the company for the next generation.

"For me personally, it's a lot of pressure and an important opportunity. I feel very well prepared. I know what I want to say. Now all I have to do is write it."

Brad explained that other department vice presidents are also scheduled to report from their various perspectives: manufacturing, employee relations, accounting, transportation, and the like. Brad explains, "Although they'll be reporting their opinions, the CEO has made it clear that the committee is eager to hear my views because enterprise risk management transcends strict departmental breakdowns. It is my job to oversee risk in every area, whether it's credit, weather, labor unrest, or interruptions in distribution."

Understand the Project

Brad's company manufactures customized novelty items such as snow globes, tote bags, key chains, and other impulse-purchase and promotional items. The company ships orders directly from its factories to retail outlets, its primary customer base. More than 40 percent of sales come from small gift stores located in tourist areas in Florida. Almost 60 percent of sales are spread among various retailers in thirteen other states. The company has two factories, one in St. Petersburg, Florida, and the other in Phoenix, Arizona. Business is good and has been growing at almost 8 percent per year for the past seven years. As Brad explains, "In order to sustain this rate of growth, we need to expand our manufacturing capabilities.

"The board of directors has decided that neither outsourcing the manufacturing nor moving the function offshore is the right move. The directors believe that outsourcing requires a set of skills we don't have and that maintaining product quality offshore is too dicey. The board decided to use the same expansion strategy that the company has used for more than eighty years—to own and operate its own manufacturing facilities.

"A team was put together to investigate options, and after six months, it recommended three options: Athens, Georgia; a second Florida location, this one outside Jacksonville; and Bushnell, Illinois, a small town about six hours' drive south of Chicago. I was told to recommend a location from a risk management perspective. I don't know which location my peers in distribution, transportation, finance, quality control, marketing, sales, and employee relations plan to recommend—they have their own data and standards. But I sensed that the prevailing view among members of the executive committee is that we should go with the Florida location. We're a Florida corporation, so it's loyal to go with what we know. According to my data, however, that's not the smartest move.

"My recommendation that we select Georgia for the new factory location is not based on my personal preference; it's an educated opinion. My analysis is objective and comprehensive, whereas I think other departments may use more limited assessments.

"In my view, different risks require different methods of evaluation, and trying to use only one method of analysis may create a false sense of security. Also, for some risks, like worker comp claims, a lot of historical data exist, whereas for other risks, like those associated with building a new factory, no such data might exist. Additionally, some risks, such as fraud, can't be methodically analyzed.

"I have spent three months identifying which data we need to look at in order to evaluate risk properly and then researching the data. I created a weighted evaluation tool known in my industry as a stochastic simulation, and based on my analysis using this tool, it is my view that we should build our new factory in Georgia."

Consider the Data

Brad explained that there are several factors that need to be discussed in his report.

"Transportation interruptions can affect our delivery commitments. Hurricanes in Florida and Georgia and blizzards in Illinois have to be considered. Some states have a greater skilled labor pool and some states are more management friendly than others. We're a nonunion company, so we need to consider the labor environment. Also, zoning regulations may impact growth. We have to ask how likely it is that changes to zoning laws might inhibit our expansion plans. Likewise, taxation policies: We have to evaluate how likely it is that taxes will increase. I spent some time talking with fire marshals trying to evaluate the risk of fire in each location. I learned that in arid, remote regions of the country, the risk of fire is greater than in wetter, more urban areas. Theft, like fraud, is very hard to predict. But certain geographic areas do seem to have higher rates of theft than other areas.

"I also assessed the costs of standard coverage. Certain regions are more expensive than others for standard insurance policies such as vehicle and workers' compensation coverage. Even if we self-insure, this criterion is a fair measure of risk."

Brad plans to attach to his report a printout of the stochastic simulation (a complex risk management analysis model that assigns probabilities and thus provides a more complete picture of the probable impact of future events). He explains, "I want the report to be no more than one page in length and both easy to read and easy to understand—period. When writing about insurance, it's easy to drift into statistics and complex, technical terminology. I want the executive committee members to be able to scan my report and 'get it.'"

STEP ONE: GET YOUR THOUGHTS IN ORDER

The first step in writing is to get an overview of your writing challenge. What do you need to accomplish, whom do you need to reach, and what obstacles must you overcome in order to succeed?

Set a Clear Objective

Brad's first task was to answer the question "What do I want my readers to do as a result of reading this report?"

EXERCISE 25: *Write an Objective*

Before reading Brad's objective, try writing your own. If you were Brad, writing a one-page report for an in-person presentation to the executive committee, how would you state your objective? What would you want the committee to do as a result of reading your report and listening to your presentation?

What did you decide? How did you state your objective?

Here's what Brad wrote:

To accept my recommendation without further analysis.

Note that Brad didn't focus on passive objectives such as being understood, thanked, or respected. He went for action.

Analyze Your Audience

You're now ready to analyze your audience by considering their personalities and by using the Formality Index. You might want to turn back to Chapter One and review the personality models (page 7) and the Formality Index (page 12) in order to complete the next step.

Identify the Personality Mix

Recognizing which personality or personalities you're trying to reach allows you to understand your target readers' needs and interests and to focus on vocabulary that's likely to satisfy them.

EXERCISE 26: *Analyze Personality*

Consider members of a senior executive committee. You can't know these individuals, of course, but for the purpose of this exercise, speculate on the kinds of people you would expect to comprise Brad's audience.

What do you think? What personality mix would you expect to find in the members of this midsize manufacturing company's senior executive committee?

If you said every personality type, you're probably right. That's almost always what you find in a mixed group. Remember, when you determine that your audience includes all personality types, start by addressing the Producers and then include everyone else.

Brad said, "In thinking about personality, most of the senior executives are pretty aggressive and technical in orientation—they're Producers and Data Collectors. But there are others on the committee who aren't technical or aggressive at all. I'm thinking of the senior vice president for new product development. He's responsible for new ideas, and he's really creative and fun—he's obviously an Optimist. And the senior VP of human resources, she's got some Data Collector in her, but she's also strongly an Accommodator. I decided that I needed to start by appealing to the Producers, followed by the other personality types."

How Formal Should the Communication Be?

In order to assess the appropriate level of formality for Brad's report, you need to consider his position within the company and his feelings about his selection of Georgia as the recommended factory site.

Brad has worked for his company in positions of increasing responsibility for six years. He is pleased with his work on this project and confident of his recommendation—he thinks the data supports the choice of Georgia. Furthermore, Brad believes that if the committee accepts his recommendation, it will be a good decision for the corporation now and into the future. He is aware, however, that several committee members prefer Jacksonville because they're loyal to their home state.

"Jacksonville isn't a bad choice," he explains. "It's just not the best choice. And it's my job to make that point inarguable."

EXERCISE 27: *Use the Formality Index*

With that background, put yourself in Brad's shoes and consider the proper level of formality by answering the three questions discussed in the model (see page 12). What score do you come up with?

Brad explained, "This exercise was interesting to me. I was certain that my score would indicate that the report should be quite formal, but what I came to realize is that *I'm* quite formal, so my inclination is that formal is always the best approach. Actually, when I calculated the score, I realized that I was wrong—I'd been looking at the situation only through my own perspective. The facts support a less formal approach.

"Specifically, I know the committee members well and personally. We're not best friends, but we have mutual respect for one another, and we've all worked together for years, so I scored the first question about how well I know them a 4. I'm below them all in rank, but I'm pretty senior within the company, so I scored the second question a 2.5. I am absolutely delivering good news. My arguments are compelling. I ranked that question a 5. Tally them up and my score totals 11.5, quite informal. It was good for me to know that an informal approach was appropriate."

Use the Matrix of Persuasion to Identify Obstacles

The Matrix of Persuasion helps you understand what you need to accomplish in your communication. Is your audience on your side or not? Are they able to do as you ask or do they lack the requisite resources?

EXERCISE 28: *Understand Your Overall Writing Assignment*
Consult Exhibit 1.1 (page 21) to refresh your memory as you determine which quadrant Brad's project is in.

Are the committee members likely to be on Brad's side? Can they do as he asks? How did you assess Brad's writing challenge?

Brad said, "Some members are on my side—they want what's best for the company. Some others aren't on my side, although they probably wouldn't see it that way. But I know that a couple of people are pretty entrenched in their views—and their view is that they want Jacksonville. There's no question that opening a new factory has wide acceptance in the company, but some people have preconceived ideas about which site is best.

"The committee has the resources it needs to do as I ask—we have the money, expertise, and time necessary to open a factory in Georgia; as committee members, each has the authority.

"That means that my report was going to be in the Easy quadrant when I considered some members of the committee, but that I needed to be persuasive for others. That gave me something to think about. As a Data Collector myself, I tend to be very matter-of-fact. I lay things out and expect a rational response. I recognized, however, that that approach wouldn't work in this case. I needed to be more persuasive than methodical."

How does your analysis compare to Brad's? Did you conclude that there was a mixed audience? Is it clear to you why, in some circumstances, a strong presentation of facts is not enough? As Brad recognized, preconceived opinions can be difficult to overcome. Don't assume that all people will make decisions based on rational factors. Do what Brad did: Analyze the situation objectively.

STEP TWO: CREATE A DRAFT ON PAPER
(OR ON YOUR COMPUTER)

Once you're armed with knowledge about what you need to accomplish and how you'll achieve it, you're ready to prepare a draft. In order to create a first draft, you need to select an organizational structure.

EXERCISE 29: *Select an Organizational Structure*

Of the nine organizational structures detailed in Chapter Two (see page 26), five are useful to convey positive information. Given that Brad had stated that his recommendation is good news, he knew that he would select one of those five. As you review them, remember your goal: *to persuade the executive committee to adopt your recommendation without further analysis.*

1. chronology
2. category
3. PAR (problem [or opportunity]/action/results)
4. Q&A
5. visual layout

Which structure do you think is best?

Each of the five structures would work; there is no one best solution. Consider how each alternative might be used:

1. If past history would be a useful predictor of future risk, it might make sense to use the chronology structure. However, given that Brad said risk factors such as fraud and theft defy prediction, this structure might be of limited value.
2. Listing the categories of risk might help Brad make his points.
3. PAR is always a good alternative when you need to be persuasive.
4. Q&A would allow Brad to highlight certain compelling points by posing carefully phrased questions.
5. The data summary might well be displayed using a visual layout. However, Brad wants his report to be only one page in length.

Based on the above analysis, most of us would have narrowed our alternatives to category, PAR, and Q&A. Did you?

Here's what Brad said: "I decided to use a combination. The summary statistics that I planned to attach would be organized by category. For the report itself, I decided to start with a PAR paragraph, followed by Q&A. I thought it would work well."

Generate Your Start and End Points

The Hub & Spokes model helps you take what's in your head and put it on paper, and it's an efficient way to begin to draft your communications. You'll recall from Chapter Two that you start by putting a summary of your objective and audience assessment in a center circle. Then, with the Matrix of Persuasion and organizational structure in mind, and using vocabulary targeting your readers' personalities, you write down whatever comes into your mind.

EXERCISE 30: *Use the Hub & Spokes Model*

Draw a circle in the center of a sheet of paper and write a summary of your objective and audience analysis inside. Focus on the key words that will affect your targeted personality types, the desired level of formality, your goal to persuade or educate, and the organizational structure you've selected. Once you're ready to concentrate, draw spokes out from the center circle and jot notes to yourself.

Take as long as you need, stopping only when you're out of ideas. When you're done, look for your most important point. That's likely to be your starting point. Your conclusion will be a summary point.

Your Hub & Spokes model will differ, of course, from Brad's. And while you may lack his technical expertise and the details behind his recommendation, you can still use the Hub & Spokes model to get your thoughts down on paper.

Were you able to jot down relevant thoughts? What came to your mind? Take a look at Brad's Hub & Spokes model (Figure 8.1) and read his comments. "I was struck by two things," Brad explained. "First, I wrote the word 'diversify' twice. Second, I found myself in a defensive position, as if I was going to be attacked for not recommending Jacksonville. If I came across as defensive during my presentation, I would weaken my performance, so I decided that I needed to win the committee's respect for my analytical process before I explained the results.

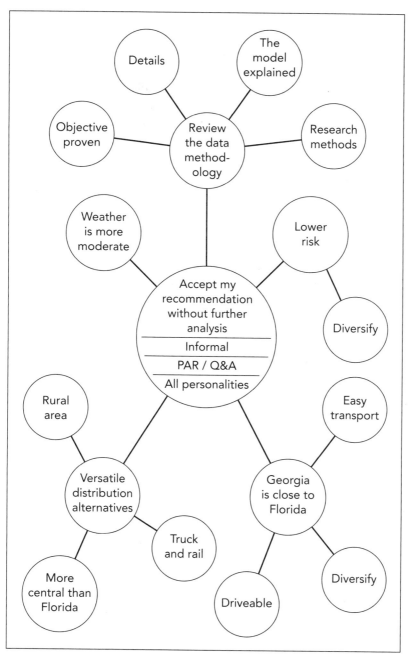

Figure 8.1 Brad's Hub & Spokes Model

"That suggested that I should start with a review of my methodology. The summary point is that Georgia is, overall, a lower-risk choice than the two alternatives. I decided that that should be my ending point.

"This exercise alerted me to a potential problem so that I could anticipate it, helped me identify my starting and ending points, and clarified the importance of constructing my report to persuade, not merely inform. Very useful."

Some people write details, others write summaries. There's no right or wrong approach. Notice that Brad didn't list specific risk factors; rather, he used the model to clarify his thinking.

Get a Draft on Paper

Armed with the knowledge of where you want to begin and where you want to end, as well as what points you want to make, you're ready to create a first draft. Remember not to worry about grammar, punctuation, or word usage at this point. Your errors will be caught and corrected as you revise.

EXERCISE 31: *Get a Draft on Paper*
In creating your first draft, you want to write with the organizational structure you've selected in mind. Are you going to adopt Brad's idea and start with a PAR paragraph followed by Q&A? Or are you going to use another structure or a combination of structures?

Remind yourself of the vocabulary that's best to use to reach Producers, as well as the words and phrases that are likely to speak to the other personality types. (If you need help, see Table 1.1 on page 9.) Focus on your starting point and get ready to put pen to paper or fingers to keyboard. Once you start, don't edit yourself, slow down, or stop until you're done or have run out of steam.

How'd you do? Did you get a draft on paper? Here's Brad's first draft:

Using proprietary stochastic simulation techniques, incorporating data collected from numerous sources of government and other public data information as well as data collected from interviews personally conducted by me and my staff, we learned without question that the bottom-line no-question absolute best choice for our new factory is

Georgia. To get a fresh view, one of my assistants met with a risk manager with no knowledge of the risks involved in doing business in either Florida or Georgia. From among the three finalists. Data is tested and proven. Objective too. Let me answer—anticipate—questions I think you're going to want to know the answers to.

Q: What data did you collect?
A: I collected data of all sorts from all sorts of data sources.

Q: Why is Georgia a better choice than Florida or Illinois?
A: It's lower risk overall and in key specific areas including weather, transport and available labor.

Q: What's the most compelling benefit of choosing Georgia?
A: Diversification. We need to mitigate against the chance of a problem in weather or labor unrest or zoning or taxation in Florida. If these problems occur in Florida, and we have more than one factory in Florida, it is easy to no doubt see the problem. Both factories is effected, not just one factory. If we have one factory only in Florida, and these factors change, not a problem. Or rather, not such a bad problem. Or actually, not likely to be such a bad problem. It's easy in retrospect to carefully understand why some of us lean toward selecting Florida but we should use objective, not subjective, criteria to make the decision. If we do that, we must go with Georgia.

Here are Brad's comments about his first draft: "I'm embarrassed to have you read it. It's terrible! But having said that, I can now say that it's also pretty good. By that I mean it provides some meat-and-potatoes content for me to work with."

What was your draft like? Brad's was just about the right length—280 words, or about one page. He made many grammatical errors, but he also made several excellent points. How did you do?

STEP THREE: REVISE FOR CLARITY

In the revision exercises that follow, use both Brad's draft and your own to give yourself two opportunities to apply the tools. Whether your first draft is close to final or whether it's rougher than Brad's, the revision tools discussed in the book will quickly help to improve it.

Maintain Your Reader Focus

The best writing is reader focused. You'll recall that the Empathy Index asks you to count references to your target readers and yourself or your organization by name, pronoun, shared interest, or implication. After rewriting your first draft to ensure a positive Empathy Index, you'll also want to confirm that your first several words, the lead, highlight a benefit and feature vocabulary likely to capture your readers' interest and attention.

EXERCISE 32: *Calculate Your Empathy Index and*
Revise to Increase Reader Focus

Calculate your first draft's Empathy Index, revise to improve it, and focus on your lead. Do the same with Brad's first draft.

Brad used italics to indicate references to his readers and underlining to indicate references to himself. See if your calculation of Brad's Empathy Index agrees with his.

Using proprietary stochastic simulation techniques, incorporating data collected from numerous sources of government and other public data information as well as data collected from interviews personally conducted by me and my staff, we learned without question that the bottom-line no-question absolute best choice for our new factory is Georgia. To get a fresh view, one of my assistants met with a risk manager with no knowledge of the risks involved in doing business in either Florida or Georgia. From among the three finalists. Data is tested and proven. Objective too. Let me answer—anticipate—questions I think you're going to want to know the answers to.

Q: What data did you collect?
A: I collected data of all sorts from all sorts of data sources.

Q: Why is Georgia a better choice than Florida or Illinois?
A: It's lower risk overall and in key specific areas including weather, transport and available labor.

Q: What's the most compelling benefit of choosing Georgia?

A: Diversification. We need to mitigate against the chance of a problem in weather or labor unrest or zoning or taxation in Florida. If these problems occur in Florida, and we have more than one factory in Florida, it is easy to no doubt see the problem. Both factories is effected, not just one factory. If we have one factory only in Florida, and these factors change, not a problem. Or rather, not such a bad problem. Or actually, not likely to be such a bad problem. It's easy in retrospect to carefully understand why some of us lean toward selecting Florida but we should use objective, not subjective, criteria to make the decision. If we do that, we must go with Georgia.

Brad said, "There were nine references to me and my staff and nine references to the corporate entity, which I used as a measure of reader focus. So my Empathy Index totals zero. Not good enough. I noticed that I had many more reader references toward the end, in the last question, than I did in the beginning. Noticing that fact helped me understand how to rewrite.

"Thinking about the lead, I realized that I had buried the words *bottom-line*. I decided to move those words up into the lead as a tactic to reach the Producers. Only after summarizing the bottom line would I talk about my methodology. Explaining my research process would appeal to Data Collectors, so I wanted to do it pretty early on. I decided to add a comment that the research required creativity to reach the Optimists, and mentioning that we assessed whether the climate was supportive of labor would appeal to Accommodators."

Go ahead and revise Brad's draft, then read Brad's revision.

After careful review, the bottom line is that the best site choice for our new factory is Georgia. To get a fresh view, one of my assistants met with a risk manager with no knowledge of the risks involved in doing business in either Florida or Georgia. My analysis used proprietary stochastic simulation techniques, incorporating data collected from numerous sources of government and other public data information as well as data collected from interviews. Designing the model required creativity and diligence. From among the three finalists. Data is tested and proven. Objective too. Let me answer—anticipate—questions I think you're going to want to know the answers to.

Q: What data did you collect?

A: I collected data of all sorts from all sorts of data sources.

Q: Why is Georgia a better choice than Florida or Illinois?

A: It's lower risk overall and in key specific areas including weather, transport and available labor as well as a positive labor climate.

Q: What's the most compelling benefit of choosing Georgia?

A: Diversification. We need to mitigate against the chance of a problem in weather or labor unrest or zoning or taxation in Florida. If these problems occur in Florida, and we have more than one factory in Florida, it is easy to no doubt see the problem. Both factories is effected, not just one factory. If we have one factory only in Florida, and these factors change, not a problem. Or rather, not such a bad problem. Or actually, not likely to be such a bad problem. It's easy in retrospect to carefully understand why some of us lean toward selecting Florida but we should use objective, not subjective, criteria to make the decision. If we do that, we must go with Georgia.

What do you think? How did you revise Brad's draft? What's your new Empathy Index? Brad said, "I know it needs more work, but I didn't want to get confused, so I focused only on the opening paragraph and added the reference to a positive labor environment."

Using italics to indicate references to his readers and underlining to indicate references to himself, here's how Brad assessed his Empathy Index.

After careful review, the bottom line is that the best site choice for our new factory is Georgia. <u>My</u> analysis used proprietary stochastic simulation techniques, incorporating data collected from numerous sources of government and other public data information as well as data collected from interviews. To get a fresh view, one of <u>my</u> assistants met with a risk manager with no knowledge of the risks involved in doing business in either Florida or Georgia. Designing the model required creativity and diligence. From among the three finalists. Data is tested and proven. Objective too. Let <u>me</u> answer—anticipate—questions <u>I</u> think *you're* going to want to know the answers to.

Q: What data did <u>you</u> collect?
A: <u>I</u> collected data of all sorts from all sorts of data sources.

Q: Why is Georgia a better choice than Florida or Illinois?
A: It's lower risk overall and in key specific areas including weather, transport and available labor as well as a positive labor climate.

Q: What's the most compelling benefit of choosing Georgia?
A: Diversification. We need to mitigate against the chance of a problem in weather or labor unrest or zoning or taxation in Florida. If these problems occur in Florida, and we have more than one factory in Florida, it is easy to no doubt see the problem. Both factories is effected, not just one factory. If we have one factory only in Florida, and these factors change, not a problem. Or rather, not such a bad problem. Or actually, not likely to be such a bad problem. It's easy in retrospect to carefully understand why some of us lean toward selecting Florida but we should use objective, not subjective, criteria to make the decision. If we do that, we must go with Georgia.

Brad identified nine references to his readers and six references to himself. "I improved it a lot, I think. My Empathy Index is now a positive three."

Work on your draft to improve your Empathy Index. Remember, the more reader focused, the better.

Close Your Communications Well

Because last lines get read and remembered, it's important that you close your communications well. Your last statement should be benefit oriented and memorable. You'll also want to consider whether a P.S., addendum, appendix, enclosures, or attachments would enhance your document.

EXERCISE 33: *Add a Snappy Close*
Consider how Brad ends his report:

It's easy in retrospect to carefully understand why some of us lean toward selecting Florida but we should use objective, not subjective, criteria to make the decision. If we do that, we must go with Georgia.

What do you think? Is it benefit oriented and memorable? Brad said, "It's pretty clear and the text anticipates an argument some committee members might make, which I think is good. The fact that the last line is short helps make it memorable. But it's not benefit oriented. I can do better."

Rewrite your conclusion if you think it needs improvement, then take a crack at making Brad's close more benefit oriented.

Were you able to improve the two conclusions? Which benefits did you highlight? Here's Brad's revision:

It's easy to understand why some of us lean toward selecting Florida but we should use objective, not subjective, criteria to make the decision. If we do that, we must conclude that the site with the highest profit potential at the lowest risk is Georgia.

Brad said, "I'm so glad I went through this process! If I hadn't, I might never have thought to mention profit potential and to remind them that Georgia offered the lowest overall risk. Looking at it now, I can't believe that I forgot to mention profit—because, after all, that is the bottom line: the lower the risk, the higher the profit potential."

Do you see Brad's point? By thinking about the ending of your communications, you're able to highlight, summarize, or restate key points.

Add Specificity to Enhance Credibility

Numbers and examples aid comprehension and believability. The more specific the examples, facts, statistics, and numbers you can integrate into your text, the more credible your communications will be.

EXERCISE 34: *Add Specificity*

In your own draft, and in Brad's, look for opportunities to add examples, numbers, or facts. Because your work on Brad's report is speculative in nature, feel free to make up likely numbers or statistics. The goal of this exercise isn't to belabor the details; rather, it is to ensure that you understand the importance of adding specificity and to be certain you know where and how to integrate examples and numbers.

How many specific references did you add to your own draft and to Brad's? Here's Brad's revision:

After careful comparison of the three site options, the bottom line is that the best choice for our new factory is Georgia. My analysis used proprietary stochastic simulation techniques, incorporating data collected from over one hundred sources, from the government and other public sources to interviews. To get a fresh view, one of my assistants met with a risk manager with no knowledge of the risks involved in doing business in either Florida or Georgia. Designing the model required creativity and diligence. All data is tested and proven by fact checkers verifying the information from additional sources. Objective too. Let me answer—anticipate—questions I think you're going to want to know the answers to.

Q: What data did you collect?
A: I collected over five hundred separate facts from all sorts of data
   sources.

Q: Why is Georgia a better choice than Florida or Illinois?
A: It's lower risk overall and in key specific areas including weather, transport and available labor as well as a positive labor climate.

Q: What's the most compelling benefit of choosing Georgia?
A: Diversification. We need to mitigate against the chance of a problem in
   weather or labor unrest or zoning or taxation in Florida. If these problems occur
   in Florida, and we have more than one factory in Florida, it is easy to no doubt
   see the problem. Both factories is effected, not just one factory. It's easy to
   understand why some of us lean toward selecting Florida but we should use
   objective, not subjective, criteria to make the decision. If we do that, we must
   conclude that the site with the highest profit potential at the lowest risk is
   Georgia.

Here's what Brad said about his revision. "I realized that I had already used examples; for instance, when I listed where Georgia is lower risk and in mentioning the potential problems in Florida. All I did was add a few numbers and rewrote some sentences to highlight the data."

Step-by-step, Brad's report is getting better. How about your draft? Can you see that it, too, is better?

Focus on Your Words

As you reread your draft, think about the actual words you use. Aim to select words that satisfy the principle of FURY. You'll recall that the principle of FURY recommends that you choose words that are familiar to your readers, unless the word in question is a unique term (such as industry jargon), rich, or your favorite.

EXERCISE 35: *Select Words with FURY*
As you review both your draft and Brad's, think about what vocabulary is most familiar to people who aren't risk management experts. Also, consider whether you and Brad are using unique words or concepts that could be more simply stated. Revise the drafts with the principle of FURY in mind.

Did you find that you replaced many words? Read Brad's revision followed by his comments.

After careful comparison of the three site options, the bottom line is that the best choice for our new factory is Georgia. My analysis used proprietary stochastic simulation techniques, incorporating data collected from over one hundred sources, from the government and other public sources to interviews. To get a fresh view, one of my assistants met with a risk manager with no knowledge of the risks involved in doing business in either Florida or Georgia. Designing the model required creativity and diligence. All data is tested and proven by fact checkers verifying the information from additional sources. Objective too. Let me answer—anticipate—questions I think you're going to want to know the answers to.

Q: What data did you collect?
A: I collected over five hundred separate facts from all sorts of data sources.

Q: Why is Georgia a better choice than Florida or Illinois?
A: It's lower risk overall and in key specific areas including weather, transport and available labor as well as a positive labor climate.

Q: What's the most compelling benefit of choosing Georgia?
A: Diversification. We need to lessen our exposure to potential prob-

lems resulting from weather or labor unrest or zoning or taxation in Florida. If these problems occur in Florida, and we have more than one factory in Florida, it is easy to no doubt see the problem. Both factories is effected, not just one factory. It's easy to understand why some of us lean toward selecting Florida but we should use objective, not subjective, criteria to make the decision. If we do that, we must conclude that the site with the highest profit potential at the lowest risk is Georgia.

"I only changed one word: *mitigate*. I think *mitigate* is a little esoteric, so I rewrote the sentence using the word *lessen*. Other words, like *proprietary*, *stochastic*, and *simulation* are unique. They are technical terms and the only way, or at least the most accurate way to make my points. I decided to leave those words in."

What do you think? Did Brad make good decisions? Did you make different decisions? Remember, there's no one way to write something, so your draft is likely to differ significantly from Brad's. For example, instead of *proprietary*, perhaps you chose *custom*. Brad's point is a good one, though. "I know my audience. These senior executives know the word *proprietary*, and it's the most accurate word for the model I created, so I'm staying with it."

Ensure Your Message Is Concise, Clear, Positive, and Parallel

In your next revision, you want to make sure your sentences aren't too long, your points are explicit, your tone is upbeat, and your construction is parallel.

EXERCISE 36: *Calculate Your Average Sentence Length*
Take your time as you work with the four concepts described above to improve the drafts. Sentences, you'll recall, should average fewer than fifteen to twenty words. Identify and correct misplaced modifiers and undefined technical terminology. Look for negative sentence constructions or words and rewrite to accentuate the positive. And be certain there's consistency throughout the communication.

Did you make significant changes? Brad did. He said, "I made every one of those errors—and I spotted some other mistakes I'd made, too. I realized I had some sentence fragments, for example, that I hadn't noticed until I focused on the sentences."

The first thing Brad did was calculate his average sentence length. He counted 272 words and eighteen sentences, equaling an average sentence length of fifteen words. "Except," Brad explained, "that that included those sentence fragments. I decided I needed to rewrite the text so there were no fragments first, and then recalculate my average sentence length. While I was doing that, remembering that shorter sentences are always better than longer ones, I tried to tighten up all the sentences. In doing so, I deleted a lot of verbiage."

Here's Brad's revision:

Bottom line: Of the three site options, the best choice is Georgia. My analysis used proprietary stochastic simulation techniques. Incorporating data collected from over one hundred sources, from the government and other public sources to interviews, the design of the model required creativity and diligence. To get a fresh view, one of my assistants met with a risk manager with no knowledge of the risks involved in doing business in either Florida or Georgia. All data is tested and proven by fact checkers. Here are answers to three key questions.

Q: What data did you collect?
A: I collected over five hundred separate facts from various data sources.

Q: Why is Georgia a better choice than Florida or Illinois?
A: Georgia is a better choice because of my overall analysis; specifically, the very low exposure in areas including weather, transport and available labor make it more attractive. Also, it offers the most positive labor climate of the three alternatives.

Q: What's the most compelling benefit of choosing Georgia?
A: Diversification. We are vulnerable to weather or labor unrest or zoning or taxation problems in Florida. If these problems occur in Florida, and we have more than one factory there, it is easy to no doubt see the problem. Both factories are effected, not just one factory. It's easy

to understand why some of us lean toward selecting Florida but we should use objective, not subjective, criteria to make the decision. If we do that, we must conclude that the site with the highest profit potential at the lowest risk is Georgia.

Brad found himself correcting several grammatical errors at the same time that he worked to shorten sentences. Brad's latest version dropped from 272 words to 249 words, a reduction of more than 8 percent. There are eighteen sentences. If you divide 272 words by eighteen sentences, you get an average sentence length of a little over fifteen words. Brad said, "That's great."

How about your draft? What's your average sentence length? If it's longer than twenty words, did you rewrite to lower your average?

EXERCISE 37: *Make It Clear*

The next task is to look for misplaced modifiers and undefined jargon or technical terminology. Did you find any? If so, correct them.

Brad said, "Rereading the sentence about getting a fresh view, I realized that there was a misplaced modifier. Of course the risk manager knew about doing business in Florida and Georgia; it was my assistant who lacked knowledge. I revised the sentence to read: 'To get a fresh view, one of my assistants with no knowledge of the risks involved in doing business in either Florida or Georgia met with a risk manager.' Also, I realized that saying that the data is tested and proven by fact checkers was inaccurate. What they were doing was verifying the accuracy of the data, not testing it or proving it. Finally, I realized that the term 'stochastic simulation,' while accurate, is technical. I had decided to leave the term in because it was precise. I still thought that was the right decision. I thought it was important that the committee know the depth of analysis I performed. I had already decided to add an attachment showcasing the stochastic simulation; now I decided to add another page explaining how it works."

Brad amended the sentence in question as follows:

My analysis used proprietary stochastic simulation techniques (see attached).

The only other change Brad made was to replace the words *tested and proven* with *verified*.

All data is verified by fact checkers.

Did you make any other changes to Brad's version? How about to your own draft?

EXERCISE 38: *Confirm That It's Positive*

Read both versions, your own and Brad's, to confirm that the message is delivered in a positive manner. If you discover a negative construction, rewrite it to make it positive.

Did you find any negative language? If so, did you rewrite the words or phrases to make them positive in tone? Brad did. He said, "I found it very interesting. I was able to turn around the negative tone of the last answer and in doing so made the communication much stronger."

Brad noted that phrases and words such as "we are vulnerable" and "problems" alerted him to the negative tone. Also, he realized that the reference to his assistant's lack of knowledge highlighted a negative fact: ignorance. He decided that the entire sentence could be deleted. Here's his revision:

Diversification. Diversification allows us to reduce our vulnerability to weather or labor unrest or zoning or taxation issues in Florida. If these events occur in Florida, and we have more than one factory there, it is easy to no doubt see the problem.

"I decided to keep the word *problem* at the end for emphasis," Brad said. "But replacing the first reference to 'problems' with the word *issues* and the second reference with the word *events* was a good move on my part, I think. Weather, for example, is an event, not necessarily a problem."

Ensure Consistency in Structure

Consistency is a hallmark of professionalism. From bulleted lists to sentence structure, it's important that your writing adhere to the principles of parallel construction that were discussed in Chapter Five.

EXERCISE 39: *Maintain Parallel Construction*

Read the drafts, looking for inconsistencies within sentences and within sections. If you find any, revise the writing so that there is consistency throughout.

Did you notice any inconsistencies in the two drafts? Brad did. He explained, "I used the word *or* too much in one sentence. Also, using *or* was inconsistent because previously I'd used commas. Once I rewrote that sentence, I realized that I should use the word *and*, not *or*, in any case. I also decided that I needed to add the word *potential*."

Here's the original sentence:

Diversification allows us to reduce our vulnerability to weather or labor unrest or zoning or taxation issues in Florida.

Here's Brad's revision:

Diversification allows us to reduce our vulnerability to potential weather, labor unrest, zoning, and taxation issues in Florida.

What do you think? Don't you agree that it's better?

Check Your Grammar, Punctuation, Word Usage, and Capitalization

In order to produce professional communications, you need to adhere to the rules of grammar that apply to business writing, ensure your punctuation is correct and consistent, verify that you're using the proper words, and capitalize correctly.

EXERCISE 40: *Proofread for Perfection*

In the last chapter you learned to be vigilant in proofing your work so that your documents are correct before they leave your office. Now review your draft and Brad's, correcting any errors you find.

Did you find many errors? Brad did. He said, "I found all sorts of errors. I had subject/verb agreement, word usage, and grammar issues." Here are the errors Brad identified and his comments.

1. All data is verified by fact checkers.

"I revised the verb to maintain the past tense," Brad explained.

All data was verified by fact checkers.

Note that "data," from the Latin *datum,* can be treated as either singular or plural. However, in the usage above, as in most scientific and research usage, the word *data* is used as a collective noun referring to a body of work, and as such is properly treated as singular.

2. Here are answers to three key questions.

Brad said, "I should have caught this earlier, but I didn't. This sentence should be a separate paragraph."

3. I collected over five hundred separate facts from various data sources.

"I decided to remove the reference to myself from the sentence," Brad said. "The sentence became passive in construction, but I decided that it was more important to highlight the impressive number of facts rather than the fact that it was I who collected them."

Over five hundred separate facts from various data sources were collected.

4. Georgia is a better choice because of my overall analysis; specifically, the very low exposure in areas including weather, transport and available labor make it more attractive.

"It occurred to me that this sentence was unclear. I decided to simplify it. I also decided that I needed to rework it in order to clarify what kinds of exposure I was talking about. I replaced the words *very* and *areas* because they're weak. I corrected the punctuation by adding a comma before the word *and,* and changed *transport* to *transportation.* I ended up reworking the entire sentence. The amazing part to me was that I didn't catch these errors until I focused on the grammar, punctuation, and word usage."

Georgia is the best choice because of the low risk of business interruptions resulting from weather, transportation, and labor.

5. Also, it offers the most positive labor climate of the three alternatives.

"I decided that this sentence was redundant, and so I deleted it. I was surprised that I hadn't recognized the redundancy when I was focused on conciseness and clarity, but I hadn't. Rereading helped me spot it."

6. Diversification allows us to reduce our vulnerability to potential weather, labor unrest, zoning, and taxation issues in Florida.

"It occurred to me that I was missing some words in this sentence, and that without them my meaning was unclear. Also, in this series, the word *or* should be used, not *and*."

Diversification allows us to reduce our vulnerability to the potential of weather, labor unrest, zoning, or taxation issues occurring in Florida.

7. If these events occur in Florida, and we have more than one factory there, it is easy to no doubt see the problem. Both factories are effected, not just one factory.

"There's a split infinitive here, a wrong word, and the sentence construction is awkward. I rewrote the sentence."

If any of these events occur in Florida, and we have two factories there, both of them would be affected, and thus our potential exposure would be doubled.

8. It's easy to understand why some of us lean toward selecting Florida but we should use objective, not subjective, criteria to make the decision.

"In looking to correct the punctuation error, I decided to simplify this sentence."

We should use objective, not subjective, criteria to make our decision.

Note that if you wanted to correct the punctuation error of the original sentence, it would read: "It's easy to understand why some of us lean toward selecting Florida, but we should use objective, not subjective, criteria to make the decision."

What do you think? Did Brad catch all the errors? What do you think of his fixes? Remember, there's always more than one way to write something well.

Here's how his latest version reads:

Bottom line: Of the three site options, the best choice is Georgia. My analysis used proprietary stochastic simulation techniques (see attached). Incorporating data collected from over one hundred sources, from the government and other public sources to interviews, the design of the model required creativity and diligence. All data was verified by fact checkers.

Here are answers to three key questions.

Q: What data did you collect?
A: Over five hundred separate facts from various data sources were collected.

Q: Why is Georgia a better choice than Florida or Illinois?
A: Georgia is the best choice because of the low risk of business interruptions resulting from weather, transportation, and labor.

Q: What's the most compelling benefit of choosing Georgia?
A: Diversification. Diversification allows us to reduce our vulnerability to the potential of weather, labor unrest, zoning, or taxation issues occurring in Florida. If any of these events occur in Florida, and we have two factories there, both of them would be affected, and thus our potential exposure would be doubled. We should use objective, not subjective, criteria to make our decision. If we do that, we must conclude that the site with the highest profit potential at the lowest risk is Georgia.

Brad was pleased with his revision. "It ended up being a lot more concise than the previous version. There are now 196 words and fifteen sentences, so my average sentence length is just over thirteen words. My Empathy Index was good, too. I had only two references to myself, but there were eight references to the corporation or the committee members; that's a score of positive six."

Confirm That Your Document Is Visually Appealing

Look at your document through your readers' eyes. Is it neat and easy to follow? If you're sending an E-mail, does it look like it was dashed off in a hurry, or does it convey a professional image? Regarding this example, Brad said, "I printed the report and attachments on letterhead, added a cover sheet, and thought it looked great."

Read It with a Critical Eye

Even if you only have minutes to conceive, draft, revise, and produce a finished message, take a breather before your final read through. Time allows you to read it with a fresh perspective, and you're likely to spot errors you might not have caught otherwise.

Brad said, "I didn't realize that I hadn't mentioned the Illinois site even once until my final read through. Only then did I notice that my closing paragraph on diversification needed to refer to Illinois, too. I'm convinced that taking the breather saved the day. I also revised the first paragraph to streamline the resource listing."

Here are Brad's original paragraphs:

Bottom line: Of the three site options, the best choice is Georgia. My analysis used proprietary stochastic simulation techniques (see attached). Incorporating data collected from over one hundred sources, from the government and other public sources to interviews, the design of the model required creativity and diligence. All data was verified by fact checkers.

Diversification. Diversification allows us to reduce our vulnerability to the potential of weather, labor unrest, zoning, or taxation issues occurring in Florida. If any of these events occur in Florida, and we have two factories there, both of them would be affected, and thus our potential exposure would be doubled. We should use objective, not subjective, criteria to make our decision. If we do that, we must conclude that the site with the highest profit potential at the lowest risk is Georgia.

Here are Brad's final revisions:

Bottom line: Of the three site options, the best choice is Georgia. My analysis used proprietary stochastic simulation techniques (see attached). Incorporating data collected from over one hundred government and other public sources and interviews, the design of the model required creativity and diligence. All data was verified by fact checkers.

Diversification. Diversification allows us to reduce our vulnerability to the potential of weather, labor unrest, zoning, or taxation issues occurring in other states. If any of these events occur in Florida, and we have two factories there, both of them would be affected, and thus our potential exposure would be doubled. Just as we've had a hard time responding nimbly to problems in Arizona, so, too, would we have difficulty responding to any of these problems occurring in Illinois.

We should use objective, not subjective, criteria to make our decision. If we do that, we must conclude that the site with the highest profit potential at the lowest risk is Georgia.

Brad took the time to carefully analyze his report, and the net result was that he produced an excellent communication that was clear and persuasive—in other words, a message that's likely to achieve his objective.

The ability to write well is crucial to business success. In this chapter you've put all the tools to work and you've seen how they help you improve your writing. Use them to write more clearly and persuasively—and to achieve your communication objectives more easily and in less time.

The writing process discussed in this book works. Use it regularly and your communications will be more likely to succeed. While the steps may seem a bit cumbersome at first, through practice they will become second nature, like driving a car. In the beginning the steps, procedures, techniques, and models will need to be consciously summoned; over time, they'll become automatic, like breathing—you won't think about using them because the process will have become so easy and natural.

Until you're able to use the process seamlessly, you may need to review some of the tools, such as the principle of FURY or the Matrix of Persuasion, while others, such as the Empathy Index or calculating average sentence length, may be more easily assimilated. But before you know it, using all the tactics described in this book will seem innate, a skill you won't be able to recall not having.

As you become more comfortable with the tools you've learned in this book, you'll discover that in addition to improving the quality of your writing, the writing process itself requires less time. In the midst of a busy workday, you'll be able to organize your thoughts, get a draft on paper, and revise it for clarity quickly and with confidence. Your communications will inspire, persuade, influence, and motivate.

Streamline Your Text

WRITE LEAN

Sometimes, business writing reads like a holdover from another age, sounding overly formal, even archaic. If your goal is write in a professional but conversational manner, you need to avoid cumbersome words and phrases. Arcane writing slows down and may even confuse your readers. Anytime readers have to pause and think about your meaning, you risk losing their attention.

Simplify Your Writing

As you scan the list of words and phrases below on the left, consider replacing them with the simpler alternatives suggested on the right. The principle of FURY, discussed in Chapter Four, highlighted the importance of using familiar and easy-to-understand words.

Instead of	Consider Using
abbreviate	shorten
accelerate	speed up
accompany	go with
accomplish	do, finish
accordingly	so
accumulate	gather
accurate	correct, exact, right
achieve	do, succeed
acquaint with	tell, inform
acquire	get, buy

Instead of	Consider Using
additional	more, other
adjacent	next to
advantageous	helpful
anticipate	expect
a number of	some, about
apparent	clear
approximate(ly)	some, more than
as a means of	to
as per	as
ask a question	ask
assistance	help
at the present time	now
at this point in time	now
be advised that	(avoid this phrase altogether)
be responsible for	handle, do
by means of	by, with
basically	(avoid)
comply with	do, follow
comprise	form, include
concerning	about
consequently	so
concur	agree
constitutes	is, forms
contains	has
contribute	give
demonstrate	show, tell
designate	appoint, choose, pick, select
determine	decide, figure out
discontinue	stop
disseminate	issue, send, spread
due to the fact that	since
eliminate	cut, drop
enclosed please find	enclosed

Instead of	**Consider Using**
encounter	meet
endeavor	try
establish	prove, show, set up
evaluate	check, test
evident	clear, obvious
facilitate	help
failed to	didn't, neglected
feasible	can be done
final	last
finalize	complete, finish
for a period of	for
for the purpose of	because
forward	attach, enclose, send
identical	equal, same
implement	do
in accordance with	by, following, under
in addition	also
in an effort to	to
inasmuch as	since
in a timely manner	by the deadline, on time, promptly
in conjunction with	with
indicate	show, tell
indication	sign
initial	first
initiate	start, undertake
in lieu of	instead of
in order to	to
in regard to	about, regarding
in the course of	during, in, when
in the event that	if, when
it is essential that	must
join together	join

Instead of	**Consider Using**
minimize	decrease, reduce
necessitate	cause, need
no later than	by
notify	tell
numerous	many, most
parameters	boundaries, limits
pertaining	about, on
per your request	as you asked
plan ahead	plan
point in time	now
previously	before, earlier
prior to	before, earlier
provided that	if
recapitulate	sum up
render	give, offer
remuneration	pay, wages
repeat again	repeat
requirement	need
solicit	ask
subsequent	later, next
subsequently	after, then
sufficient	enough
terminate	end, stop
there are	(avoid)
therefore	so
therein	there
there is	(avoid)
timely	prompt (or specify)
utilize	use
whereas	since
with reference to	about
with the exception of	except for

The Correct Use of Prepositions

CORRECT PREPOSITION USE ENHANCES PROFESSIONALISM

Using prepositions properly is a hallmark of professionalism in both speech and writing, but learning which preposition to use in which circumstance requires memorization.

This appendix does not attempt to list all prepositions in all applications. Rather, it will clear up some areas of confusion (e.g., The sale is extended *to* September 1st vs. The sale is extended *through* September 1st).

Certain Words Require Certain Prepositions

Certain words must be followed by certain prepositions in order to achieve clarity. Learning these combinations will help you conform to professional standards in business writing. The following list of common combinations clarifies which preposition to use when.

account for *(to explain or justify something missing)*
account to *(to explain or justify something to someone)*

- He needs to account for his absence at the client meeting.
- He will have to account to Mr. Peterson for missing the client meeting.

agree on or upon *(arrive at an understanding)*
agree to *(go along with)*
agree with *(believe the same thing as someone else)*

- Michael and Joe have agreed on changing the schedule.
- Michael and Joe agreed to Mr. Peterson's ideas for changing the schedule.
- Michael and Joe agreed with Mr. Peterson's ideas for changing the schedule.

angry at or **about** *(irritated at or about something)*
angry with *(irritated with someone)*

- Mario was angry at the finding of the courts.
- Mario was angry with Jules for an inadequate defense.

apply for *(a job or other opportunity)*
apply to *(a person or an organization)*

- Mario decided to apply for the position of chef.
- After serving three months of the six-month sentence, Mario decided to apply for the early release program.
- Mario applied to Ms. Myerson for help in winning the parole board's approval.
- Mario applied to the new hotel for a job as chef.

compare to *(make a general comparison)*
compare with *(evaluate specific similarities and differences)*

- Harriet compared my performance to Frank's.
- When Harriet compared my performance with Frank's, she said I was better at ad libbing but not as smooth in my delivery.

convenient for *(appropriate)*
convenient to *(nearby)*

- Des Moines is convenient for all of us.
- Des Moines is convenient to Chicago.

differ about *(something)*
differ from *(something else)*
differ with *(a person)*
different from *(distinct)*
different than *(compared to)*

- We differed about research methodology, not personnel.
- My current research differs from Josie's in significant ways.
- I differ with Josie over the methodology we plan to use.
- My research is different from Josie's.
- I view it in a different way than Josie does.

knocked on *(to rap or tap on some thing)*
knocked out *(to cause to lose consciousness; slang, informal, used in business writing: to be extremely impressed)*

- Before entering, I knocked on the door.
- When I pushed open the door, it hit his head and he was knocked out.
- Slang: I was knocked out by Matthew's terrific idea.

speak to *(inform)*
speak with *(share ideas with)*

- Mr. Peterson insists on speaking to them personally about the schedule.
- Mr. Peterson hopes you'll speak with them about the schedule.

to *(up to but not including x)*
through *(up to and including x)*

- The leak spread to the chairman's office.
- The leak spread through the chairman's office.

Prepositions can be tricky. Use the above listing as a guide, so you'll be certain to avoid common pitfalls.

Index